For your reading

LONDON'S

STRANGEST TALES

HISTORIC
ROYAL PALACES

LONDON'S
STRANGEST TALES

HISTORIC ROYAL PALACES

EXTRAORDINARY BUT TRUE STORIES

IAIN SPRAGG

PORTICO

First published in the United Kingdom in 2014 by
Portico
10 Southcombe Street
London W14 0RA

An imprint of Pavilion Books Group Ltd

ISBN 9781909396470

A CIP catalogue record for this book is available from the British Library.

20 19 18 17 16 15 14
10 9 8 7 6 5 4 3 2 1

Reproduction by Rival Colour Ltd, UK
Printed and bound by 1010 Printing International Ltd, China

This book can be ordered direct from the publisher at www.anovabooks.com,
or try your local bookshop.

CONTENTS

INTRODUCTION

The Royal Family is today synonymous with the splendour and grandeur of Buckingham Palace. Iconic images of the Royals assembled on the famous balcony on the East Front on state occasions are the epitome of the British Establishment and, notwithstanding the sight of comedian Peter Kay dressed as a Beefeater on the roof of the palace during The Queen's Diamond Jubilee concert in 2012, the building remains the architectural embodiment of the monarchy.

Buckingham Palace, however, is a relatively recent addition to the royal property portfolio. Queen Victoria only picked up the keys to the place after her accession to the throne in 1837. Before her long and popular reign, the Royal Family once called five other palaces in London 'home'.

London's Strangest Tales: Historic Royal Palaces charts and celebrates the fascinating stories of this quintet of historic buildings.

Known collectively as the Historic Royal Palaces, the Tower of London, Hampton Court Palace, the Banqueting House, Kew Palace and Kensington Palace have all provided a roof over the head of royalty over the centuries. Over the last thousand years, all five have stood silent witness to British history in the making.

It was William the Conqueror who began the regal property boom in the capital, commissioning the construction of the imposing Tower of London in 1066 following his triumph at the Battle of Hastings, a victory which gave him the crown and the country. Henry VIII subsequently gave Hampton Court the royal seal of approval in 1529 when he evicted the hapless Cardinal Wolsey, while James I's desire for a London party pad was the catalyst for the building of the third incarnation of the Banqueting House in 1619. It was domestic considerations that prompted King George II to relocate his rapidly expanding family into Kew Palace in 1729, while the asthmatic William III was attracted to

Kensington 60 years later because the location was 'esteem'd with a very good air', the monarch paying £20,000 to persuade the resident owner to vacate the premises.

Each palace was to enjoy varying lengths of residential service. Parts of Kensington still house members of the Royal Family, with William, Kate and their son George the new arrivals in 2013, but all five residences eventually fell from favour. They are now preserved for the public and for prosperity by the charity Historic Royal Palaces.

The Tower of London's grisly reputation for torture and execution precedes it. It's certainly true that many a poor soul spent their final, miserable hours within the confines of its now infamous walls but the Tower's ongoing history is as intriguing as it is undeniably murderous.

From the bizarre tale of the first alcohol-assisted escape from its cells, King Haakon's voracious polar bear, the reluctant visit of Ronnie and Reggie Kray and the closely guarded arrival of the medals for the London Olympics in 2012, life at the Tower over the centuries has never been dull.

The story of Hampton Court is equally captivating. From Wolsey's unfortunate terror at the palace's eight-legged interlopers to William Shakespeare and his Globe players' Christmas sojourn, Anne Boleyn's penchant for gambling at the tennis courts and its unlikely 19th-century suffragette house guest, the palace has always been a hotbed of curios which have frequently eclipsed even Hampton's famous maze.

The Banqueting House's stint as a royal residence was as brief as it was eventful and over the years the palace has impassively observed the country's first incident of state-sponsored regicide, the surreal ritual of the monarch attempting to cure disease with a touch of the regal hand, James II's futile attempts to cling to power by mounting a weather vane on the roof of the building and the macabre arrival of the skeletal remains of Napoleon's horse.

Kew may be the most modest of our five palaces in terms of size and scope but while it lacks stature, it does not disappoint in terms of tantalising tales that include the strange story of the demolition of the first mosque ever built in Britain, an improbable mob of resident kangaroos, a very literal interpretation of Swan Lake and the superstitious 17th-century craftsmen who built the palace.

In contrast it is the litany of unusual guests, invited or sometimes otherwise, who have made their way to Kensington over the years that have lit up its unusual history. The mugger who accosted George II in the palace gardens at pistol point was most definitely intruder rather than invitee, while the American Indian chief Tomochichi who turned up for a meet-and-greet with the same monarch may have been an unusual sight in 18th-century England but was at least on the guest list.

Peter, the tragic, feral child who was unceremoniously shipped over from Germany, was another incongruous but scheduled visitor to Kensington, while the abrupt arrival of the Grim Reaper as George II sat on the royal toilet was certainly not the palace's most edifying appointment.

Sometimes the pomp and ceremony of a state occasion has spawned the surreal or the silly, as the unfortunate Persian ambassador who unwittingly insulted Charles I at Banqueting House could testify, while other intriguing palace stories arise from more private royal moments, such as Victoria's dressing-gown diplomacy at Kensington when she was informed she was the new queen on 20th June 1837.

The Historic Royal Palaces of London remain a striking depository of the nation's collective history and this book explores the most memorable and frequently comic events and incidents they have witnessed since they first opened their doors to their myriad royal occupants.

London's Strangest Tales: Historic Royal Palaces is not a definitive history of the Tower of London, Hampton Court, Banqueting House, Kew and Kensington; that is the job of more academic tomes. The pages that follow are an affectionate celebration of the lesser-known and more bizarre stories that are as much a part of the DNA of the five palaces as all the pageantry and ceremony in which they have also played such an integral part.

THE MONK WITH BLOOD
ON HIS HANDS
1078

The Tower of London has earned itself something of a bloody reputation over the centuries courtesy of some of the unspeakably nasty things inflicted on its reluctant, terrified residents. Getting banged up in the Tower was no picnic; it could be absolute murder.

Its macabre, frequently fatal history began in 1066 when William the Conqueror, fresh from roughing up the English and killing Harold at the Battle of Hastings, despatched his minions to London to start work on a new castle. The natives were restless and William wanted to show them who was the boss.

The original Tower was a timber motte-and-bailey castle, a classic Norman design. It was built on the same site that the Roman Emperor Claudius had constructed his own fortress a millennium earlier but William yearned for an even bigger and bolder architectural stick to wave at his troublesome new subjects and in 1078 he ordered the construction of a massive stone keep, the likes of which England had never seen before. That, he reasoned, would keep the buggers quiet.

The job of designing and building what was to become known as the White Tower was handed to a chap called Gundulf and here lies the rub because while his formidable keep was to acquire a gruesome reputation for torture and murder, Gundulf was actually a very religious and devout man.

A Norman monk, he nipped across the Channel after the Conquest and in 1077 he was promoted to the position of the Bishop of Rochester. A year later William asked him to get his set square and ruler out and start work on designing the imposing White Tower.

According to the medieval manuscript *Textus Roffensis*, Gundulf was 'skilled and competent at building in stone' while his biography, the imaginatively entitled *The Life Of Gundulf* written by one of the monks at Rochester, records his piety and deeply held beliefs. 'There were times when he was greatly pressed in his unremitting care of the poor,' it reads. 'Or hindered by his duties as steward, or had no place where, hidden from the eyes of men, he could spend himself before God as was his wont in prayers and tears.'

A thoroughly good egg then and not at all the kind of character who would advocate torture. Exactly what Gundulf would have made of his Tower's gory future is unknown but it's probably safe to assume he wouldn't have approved of all the slashing, whipping and beheading. Luckily for him he joined the choir invisible in 1108, long before the worst excesses were exacted on its hapless prisoners.

The White Tower was completed in 1097 and it was certainly impressive, standing 36m (118ft) high, dominating the London skyline and daring the locals to come and have a go if they thought they were hard enough. William was delighted, which couldn't be said of some of the Tower's 'guests' when they were dragged in chains into its dark and intimidating interior.

FLAMBARD'S DOUBLE FIRST
1100

People who work for Her Majesty's Revenue & Customs are not everyone's cup of tea. In truth, they regularly rank somewhere below Pol Pot, Mr Blobby and dandruff in the popularity stakes, and employees of the Tax Man are rumoured to spend most evenings talking to traffic wardens in online chat rooms.

And thus it has always been judging by the interesting story of Ranulf Flambard, the erstwhile chief tax inspector for England in the late 11th century, the Bishop of Durham and a man who boasts two contrasting claims to fame.

Flambard worked for William II ensuring the royal coffers were kept brimming with taxes but when the King was killed in 1100 by a mysteriously stray arrow on a hunting trip in the New Forest, he was succeeded by Henry I and Flambard's fortunes took something of a spectacular nosedive. Flambard had become a wealthy man in William's service but as soon Henry ascended to the throne, he was accused of extortion and imprisoned at the Tower of London.

Whether the historic distinction of becoming the Tower's first ever prisoner improved his mood is a moot point but Flambard did not have long to dwell on his misfortune as he contemplated a way of regaining his freedom.

He waited until the feast of Candelmas to affect his escape. Flambard ordered a barrel of wine and invited his guards to join him in the festivities, ensuring his captors drank freely and regularly until they were quite, quite tipsy. When his bibulous jailors were in an alcohol-induced sleep, the Bishop produced a rope which had been hidden inside the barrel of wine, tied it securely to a stone column in his cell and abseiled out the window to be met by friends waiting with horses, hastily beating a retreat to exile in Normandy.

The guards' hangovers were not improved when they learned of the breakout and such was the shock at his daring flit that one contemporary chronicler accused the bishop of witchcraft. The mechanics of his escape were of course far more prosaic but Flambard's getaway did earn him the dubious distinction as both the first man to be imprisoned at the Tower of London and the first to escape its confines successfully.

THE LAST DAYS OF LLYWELYN
1282

Anglo-Welsh relations have endured what we might euphemistically describe as a number ups and downs over the centuries but it's probably safe to say they were never more strained than in 1282 when King Edward I's forces defeated Prince Llywelyn (aka Llywelyn ap Gruffydd) at the Battle of Orewin Bridge.

The battle was the epitome of a grudge match after a decade of fighting, wrangling and bitter political manoeuvring between the leaders of the English and the Welsh and when news reached Edward that Llywelyn had been killed, the King couldn't wipe the smile off his face.

The exact circumstances of the Prince's death are disputed. Some chroniclers credit a Stephen Frankton, the 'centurion' of Ellesmere, with delivering the fatal blow while other annals name a knight called Sir Robert Brody as the man who did the deadly deed. Some reports maintain the myth that Llywelyn was slain in battle while many more insist the Prince was betrayed, tricked into believing he was to receive homage from Edward's proxy Roger Mortimer, only to be surrounded and assassinated.

Edward of course didn't give a damn about the details. Llywelyn was to be the last ruler of an independent Wales and with him out of the way, Edward could now get on with the important business of subjugating and annexing the rebellious Principality.

To do this, he had to make a very public show of his latest victory and this is where the Tower of London enters our gruesome story.

Llywelyn's post-mortem indignities began when his head was hacked off. Mortimer dutifully despatched it as a trophy to Edward at his garrison in north Wales and after it had been triumphantly displayed to the English soldiers on Anglesey, it began its journey to London and the Tower.

In the English capital the grizzly souvenir of battle was crowned with a ring of ivy, mocking the ancient Welsh prophecy that a Welshman would be anointed the ruler of Britain in London. After that it was transported on the point of a lance through the city and deposited on a spike above one of the gates of the Tower.

Edward certainly didn't do things by half and to publicly underline his new grip on power in Wales, he left Llywelyn's head on display for 15 full years. What became of it is shrouded in mystery but Llywelyn's headless body is thought to be buried at the Cistercian abbey in Abbeycwmhir.

Sadly, Llywelyn was not alone at the Tower for long. Following his death, his brother Dafydd became the leader of the Welsh and launched an ill-fated rebellion but in June 1283 he was captured, sentenced to death and finally hung, drawn and quartered. The King subsequently ordered Dafydd's head join his brother's at the Tower. You really didn't want to get on the wrong side of Edward.

ANARCHY IN THE UK
1381

The Peasants' Revolt in 14th-century England was the Medieval equivalent of the Poll Tax riots, a popular and passionate uprising against the injustices of the taxation system and a protest against the obstinate ruling classes.

In 1990 it was Margaret Thatcher who was the focus of anger but back in 1381 it was Richard II who was public enemy number one with the disgruntled populous and when the famed Wat Tyler raised an army of 10,000 rebels from Kent, Essex, Suffolk and Norfolk to march on London, the King decided it might be prudent to abandon Windsor Castle and retreat behind the reassuringly thick stone walls of the Tower of London.

Tyler and the peasants enjoyed a two-day spree of looting, ransacking and general mayhem in the Big Smoke until Richard decided it was high time for dialogue rather destruction and, to his credit, bravely left the Tower for a bit of a chin wag with Wat and the angry rebels.

It proved to be a disastrous move as the garrison at the Tower forgot to lock up after their boss had left the building, leaving the castle at the mercy of the mob. 'The king had ridden out to meet the rebels at Mile End,' recorded the writer Jean Froissart in his *Chronicles*. 'The Tower's drawbridge and portcullis gates had not been raised behind him and a mob of least 400 men stormed the castle. The men-at-arms guarding the Tower put up on resistance and the peasants shook their hands as brothers and stroked their beards in a friendly fashion.'

The sight of amicable facial hair fumbling may have been comical but Simon Sudbury, the Archbishop of Canterbury and the King's chief tax collector, failed to see the funny side as he was captured by the rebels, dragged out onto Tower Hill and summarily executed.

It was, by all accounts, a particularly grizzly end as the impromptu axe man took eight strokes before eventually decapitating his man.

At this stage, you could be forgiven for thinking the rebels had pulled off something of a coup in successfully storming the previously impregnable Tower but they did, in truth, make one major mistake which is frequently overlooked in the retelling.

The Tower was a veritable cornucopia of weaponry. The royal armoury was nothing if not well stocked and the rebels were probably extremely pleased with themselves when they pinched 20 springbald bolts for their collection. The problem was they neglected to steal any springbalds with which to fire them.

Springbalds, according to one historian, were 'terrible machines of war' and 'shot huge missiles which no armour could resist.' Think giant crossbow and you're there. They would certainly have come in very handy when Richard deployed 4,000 troops to quell the revolt, but the careless rebels were left ineffectually clutching 20 enormous arrows with absolutely no way of propelling them towards the advancing royal forces.

The rebellion was soon quashed and Wat Tyler suffered the same fate as that of the archbishop.

CHAUCER'S SECOND JOB
1389

'Jack of all trades but master of none' is a figure of speech which was first recorded in the late 16th century and is sadly an expression which has assumed negative connotations. These days we worship specialism and frown suspiciously on those with the audacity to boast more than one string to their bow.

Back in the Middle Ages however some of the country's leading figures were proud multi-taskers. Everyone had a second job and no-one thought it strange if a priest worked part-time as a tax collector or a an artist moonlighted as a funeral director.

Geoffrey Chaucer was no different. History commemorates him as the father of English literature thanks to the posthumous publication of *The Canterbury Tales* but our Geoffrey was rarely idle and also dabbled in philosophy, alchemy and astronomy when he was not penning his bawdy and comic account of pilgrimage.

He was also, more bizarrely, the man responsible for the completion of Tower Wharf on the Thames at the Tower of London. Whether Geoffrey actually had any construction qualifications is unknown but he was nonetheless appointed Clerk of the King's Works in 1389 and part of what was a diverse portfolio of work on Tower Wharf.

In truth, his new role was that of a glorified foreman but as well as overseeing repairs of Westminster Palace, St George's Chapel and Windsor Castle, he was responsible for the building of the revetment wall at the Wharf, a structure designed to absorb the tidal energy of the River Thames. In 1391 the work was finished and with the Tower now fully integrated with the river, Geoffrey could get back to his quill and parchment.

To his credit, the revetment wall stood firm until 2003 when it finally collapsed after years of subterranean weakening by tree roots.

The peckish, modern visitor to the Tower of London can choose to eat at the Perkin Reveller restaurant on the Wharf. The well-read diner will already know Perkin Reveller was the apprentice chef character in the Cook's Tale in *The Canterbury Tales*.

IMPOSTER AT THE TOWER
1491

The intriguing story of the imprisonment and subsequent disappearance of the princes in the Tower is one of the most infamous in English history, encompassing at it does bloody betrayal, Machiavellian ambition and enduring myth.

The two princes in question were Edward and his younger brother Richard, the only surviving sons of Edward IV, who were 'lodged' at the Tower of the London in 1483, by their uncle Richard, Duke of Gloucester, in preparation for Edward's coronation as King Edward V.

The 12-year-old Edward, however, never made it to Westminster Abbey for his big day. His uncle took the throne for himself, the boys mysteriously disappeared and contemporary conspiracy theorists immediately swung into action, quite understandably speculating that Richard III had quietly disposed of his unfortunate nephews, hidden their bodies in the Tower and innocently busied himself polishing his new crown. A fascinating and famous tale but there is a footnote.

In 1491 a young man landed and came ashore in Ireland and publicly announced he was Richard, the younger of Edward IV's surviving sons. He had, he claimed, escaped from the Tower after Richard's coronation eight years earlier and although Henry VII now sat on the English throne, it was he who he was the rightful and legitimate heir.

A revelation on a par with Luke discovering Darth Vader was his real father, the news of Richard's apparent resurfacing spread through the Continent like wild fire and although there was no actual evidence to back up his bold claims, a number of European monarchs exploited the uncertain situation to grind their own political and military axes with Henry.

With the support of first Mary of Burgundy, then the King of Scotland and finally Cornish rebels, Richard mounted three spectacularly unsuccessful attempts to invade England and force his claim to the throne. Each time he was forced to flee with his tail firmly between his legs. His 'luck' ran out in 1497 when he was captured by royal forces in Hampshire and, after a brief stint in chokey in Taunton, he was 'paraded through the streets [of London] on horseback amid much hooting and derision of the citizens' before being incarcerated in the Tower.

Henry had got his troublesome man but he needed to kill the myth his prisoner was really Richard. The pretender to the throne remained a rallying point for all of his many enemies and it was imperative the rumours about his legitimacy were quashed.

It was time to unpack the instruments of torture and after what must have been some excruciatingly painful treatment, 'Richard' finally confessed he was actually called Perkin Warbeck and that he hailed from Tournai in what is now modern Belgium. He had, he screamed in agony, made the whole thing up.

In a display of surprising leniency, Henry initially sentenced him to life imprisonment rather than the big sleep but after Perkin managed to escape in 1499, only to be quickly recaptured, the King's patience ran out and our audacious imposter was taken from the Tower, forced to read out a public confession and hanged at the gallows at Tyburn.

'A man is never more truthful,' wrote Mark Twain, 'than when he acknowledges himself a liar.' A sentiment which would probably have proved little solace to Warbeck as he breathed his last.

HAMPTON'S EIGHT-LEGGED EPIDEMIC
1514

Houses have always been symbols of success. The bigger the pad, the fatter the salary and ever since man emerged from the caves and tentatively began to build his own shelters, people have been indulging in a never-ending game of architectural one-upmanship.

Cardinal Wolsey was definitely a fan of residential Top Trumps as he climbed the greasy pole of English society in the early 16th century and had it not been for him, Hampton Court Palace would never have been built.

His rise from humble origins in Suffolk took him right to the top and by 1514 he was Archbishop of York and would add Lord Chancellor to his CV the following year. More importantly, he was Henry VIII's *de facto* right-hand man and Wolsey now decided he needed a lavish pad to reflect his rising star.

He opted for an old manor house in Richmond as the site for his grand design and over the next seven years, he spent 200,000 gold crowns transforming it into the nucleus of the Hampton Court we know today. The Cardinal was now the proud owner of some serious real estate.

Sadly for Wolsey, he would enjoy his resplendent new property for a mere 16 years, during which time his lavish lifestyle earned him a lot of enemies. In 1529 his bromance with Henry hit the rocks when the Cardinal failed to secure an annulment to the King's marriage to Catherine of Aragon. Wolsey was summarily stripped of office and his property and Henry gleefully helped himself to Hampton Court, beginning the palace's period of royal history and, frankly, saving the King a fortune in stamp duty and estate agent fees.

The following year the Cardinal was accused of treason and although he died from illness before he ever faced trial, it was nonetheless a spectacular and abrupt end to a political career that had shone so brightly.

The twist in the tale is that Wolsey was never particularly enamoured of Hampton Court. It was undoubtedly magnificent but it also unfortunately proved to be pied-à-terre of choice of a rare and rather large breed of spider which scared the bejeezus out of the arachnophobic Cardinal.

The eight-legged invader in question was *Tegenaria parietina* which usually lives in Continental Europe, North Africa and Asia but for reasons no-one has ever really established, also found Hampton Court a rather agreeable place to hang out. Wolsey was a nervous wreck as the uninvited guests made themselves at home and such was his fear, they became known as 'cardinal spiders'.

'There is a large breed of spiders which are found very generally in the palace of Hampton Court,' reported the 1833 edition of the *Arcana Of Science*.

'They are called there cardinals having it is supposed been first seen in Cardinal Wolsey's hall. They are full an inch in length and many of them of thickness of a finger. Their legs are about two inches long and their body covered with a thick hair.

'In running across the carpet in an evening with the shade cast from their large bodies by the light of the lamp or candle, they have been mistaken for mice and have occasioned no little alarm to some of the more nervous inhabitants of the palace.

'A doubt has even been raised whether the name of cardinal has not been given to this creature from an ancient supposition that the ghost of Wolsey haunts the place of his former glory under this shape.'

So if you see a cobweb at Hampton Court, spare a thought for the palace's first, terrified owner.

CATERING FOR THE CARNIVORES
1526

It was in the early Noughties that the dreams of carnivores worldwide came true when the Atkins Diet exploded onto the scene. Suddenly steaks and chops were *de rigueur* and anyone who wanted to lose a few pounds was actively encouraged to chomp their way through as much flesh as they fancied. Meat eaters simply couldn't believe their luck and the widespread reports of dieters' smelly breath and suspiciously odorous urine seemed a small price to pay.

Devotees of Atkins however were far from the first to favour such a predominantly meaty menu judging by the extravagant eating habits at Hampton Court during Henry VIII's reign. The King himself was renowned as a portly fella but his royal subjects who dined daily at Hampton Court with him were not exactly parsimonious themselves.

According to contemporary records, the court got through a staggering 8,200 sheep annually. They also chowed down on 2,300 deer each year and consumed 1,870 pigs. A total of 1,240 oxen and 760 calves sacrificed their lives in the name of haute cuisine while 53 wild boar were also served up, all washed down with an estimated 600,000 gallons of beer. Try getting Ocado to deliver that lot next time you order online.

Such carnivorous consumption of course demanded plenty of cooking space and Hampton Court was blessed with vast kitchens, built in 1530, to cater for the twice-daily feasts.

It was a tough gig downstairs in the hot, sweaty kitchens. Several master cooks were in charge of the multitude of dishes demanded by the monarch of the day and they were aided and abetted by a small army of yeomen and sergeants but it was frequently chaotic and deafening, prompting one Spanish dignitary visiting Hampton

Court in 1554 to describe a scene of 'veritable hells, such is the stir and bustle in them. There is plenty of beer and they drink more than would fill the Valladolid river.'

Meat though was not the only thing on the royal table and on the evidence of a menu served up to hungry Henry and Katherine of Aragon by Cardinal Wolsey in 1526, it transpires that the King, his wife and his resident courtiers were also partial to some of the more exotic fruits of the sea. It was surf and turf on the grandest of scales.

It was a mere two course meal but both sittings were enormous and included, amongst other varied nautical offerings, 'crabbes, lobsters, purpose [porpoise], calver salmon, eles with lampreys, creys [crayfish], shrympes and whyting.'

Little wonder Henry piled on the pounds later in life almost as rapidly as he acquired and discarded wives.

ANNE'S FINAL GAMBLE
1536

The story of the remarkable rise and dramatic fall of Anne Boleyn, her controversial marriage to Henry VIII and, from her husband's point of view, her expedient execution is as well documented as it is pure melodrama. Anne was Queen for less than three years and yet her name still resonates through history, feted as the woman who proved the catalyst for the schism between the Church of England and the Roman Papacy.

Anne, however, was a far more three-dimensional character than that and whether you subscribe to the theory she was an innocent victim of wider political machinations or a self-serving *femme fatale*, she continues to divide historical opinion.

What we do know is Anne really liked a flutter. She was perhaps not what we would euphemistically now call a 'problem gambler' but the long days spent at Hampton Court needed filling and Anne was certainly not averse to wile them away placing the odd bet.

Henry, of course, controlled the purse strings and she was provided with a 'small' amount of money to wager with at any one time. That 'small' amount though was the equivalent of £1,500 in today's money, so Anne was hardly making pauper's bets.

One of her favourite sports to bet on was bowls but she was no great shakes at the game and on at least one occasion Henry had to dip in the royal petty cash to cover her losses, which totalled £3,600 in current currency.

Anne's carefree days were to come to an end in 1536 when Henry, frustrated at her failure to produce a son and eager to hook up with Jane Seymour, had his minions draw up charges of adultery, incest and treason against the missus.

In early May she was arrested. Whether she feared or suspected then that it would only be a few weeks before she was beheaded at the Tower of London is unknown but contemporary reports do tell us Anne was at Hampton Court's famed indoor tennis court before she was hauled off, awaiting the result of the match on which she had just placed a bet. When the long arm of the law arrived, Anne did not protest at the injustice of her plight but rather complained that she wished to know the result of the game that she might collect her winnings.

The Queen never did find out who won. Just 17 days after her unceremonious and final exit from Hampton Court, the sword descended and her time was up.

SLEEPING BEAUTY
1546

Falling asleep at work is generally frowned on. It tends to suggest a lack of professionalism and bosses really don't like it when you have 40 winks on their time. It's a particularly bad habit if you happen to be an airline pilot, Formula One driver or heart surgeon.

Back in the 16th century however William Foxley took snoozing on the job to an unprecedented new level when he slept for 14 days and 15 nights while an employee of the Royal Mint at the Tower of London.

According to *A Survey Of London*, written by the historian John Stow and published five decades after the incident:

> 'In the year 1546, the 27th of April being Tuesday in Easter week, William Foxley potmaker for the Mint in the Tower of London, fell asleep and so continued sleeping and could not be wakened with pricking, cramping or otherwise, burning whatsoever, until the first day of the term, which was full fourteen days and fifteen nights or more for that Easter term beginneth not before seventeen days after Easter. The cause of his thus sleeping could not be known though the same was diligently searched after by the king's physicians and other learned men.'

A strange story indeed but luckily for Foxley his unexplained sleep did not result in a P45. In fact, he became so famous during his mysterious lapse into apparent unconsciousness that King Henry VIII himself couldn't resist a trip to see the Tower's comatose celebrity in person.

The history books record that when Foxley did finally awake he declared he'd only been out for a single night and was amazed to be told he'd had been in the land of nod for a fortnight. The experience had no lasting effect on his health and he worked at the Mint for a further 40 years without another impromptu lapse into long-term slumber.

Modern science has since tried to explain Foxley's bizarre tale and after architects discovered high levels of lead in Tudor pottery, the current best guess is that he was an unsuspecting victim of severe metal poisoning.

DRAMA AT HAMPTON COURT
1603

Hampton Court boasts a multitude of historical claims to fame but one of the lesser known is its illustrious theatrical past, one of just three surviving buildings to have staged productions of the plays of William Shakespeare during The Bard's own lifetime.

It was Christmas 1603 when Will and his King's Men were summoned to Hampton by James I. The king was evidently bored over the holiday period, having perhaps endured one too many game of charades with the in-laws or repeats of *Dad's Army*, and Shakespeare and his actors dutifully decamped from the Globe Theatre in town to entertain their restless monarch.

It was not though to be a one-night only gig. Shakespeare and his troupe were to stay at Hampton for three full weeks and performed a total of seven plays for James and his royal court in the Great Hall as 1603 reluctantly gave way to 1604. According to the annals, James sat through *The Comedy Of Errors, Love's Labour Lost, The Merry Wives of Windsor, Othello, Measure for Measure* and *The Merchant of Venice* (twice) during Shakespeare's impromptu residency.

We don't know whether Will himself took to the stage but it does seem he prudently decided not to perform either *Hamlet* or *Macbeth*, featuring as they famously do scenes of rather bloody regicide.

Shakespeare of course performed at many other venues in the early 17th century but his favoured theatres such as the Swan, Blackfriars, the Curtain and the original Globe have long since perished, lending Hampton Court the rare distinction as one of the last surviving scenes of his work before his death in 1616.

The other two are Gray's Inn and Middle Temple in London, the former staging a production of *The Comedy of Errors* in 1594 and the latter *Twelfth Night* eight years later.

THE AGONY OF ARABELLA

1611

Marrying in secret is invariably fraught with danger. You risk making a lifelong enemy of the new mother-in-law, you've got the headache of finding witnesses and, most significantly, you kiss goodbye to the wedding presents windfall and a deluge of Tefal toasters and Moulinex blenders.

The clandestine nuptials of William Seymour, the second Duke of Somerset, and Lady Arabella Stuart in 1610 however had even more serious repercussions.

The happy couple were fourth and sixth respectively in line to the English throne and the marriage definitely displeased King James I, who saw their union as a potential threat to his ruling dynasty. Something had to be done about the reckless lovers and the following year Seymour found himself banged up in the Tower of London while Arabella was placed under house arrest in Lambeth.

'I do assure you that nothing the State can do with me can trouble me so much as this news of your being ill doth,' Arabella wrote to her ailing husband. 'When I am troubled, I trouble you with too tedious kindness, for so I think you will account so long a letter. But, sweet sir, I speak not of this to trouble you with writing but when you please. Be well and I shall account myself happy in being. Your faithful, loving wife.'

This could have been the end of the lovers' story but they were nothing if not resourceful and a daring, double escape plan was hatched. It wasn't quite as daring as *Escape To Victory* but it initially did the trick.

Arabella gained her freedom with a spot of cross dressing, disguising herself as a man and literally walking out of her confinement. Seymour left the Tower concealed in a wood cart while his servant stayed behind, telling the guards his master was confined to his bed with a tooth ache.

The pair planned to reunite on a boat on the Thames and finally head off on honeymoon but this is where it all went pear shaped. Seymour hopped on the wrong boat and ended up *tout seul* in Flanders while Arabella was arrested just outside Calais and taken to the Tower to ensure she did not go walkabout again.

The newlyweds never saw each other again. Arabella was unable to make a second audacious escape from the King's wrath and in 1615 she died in a part of the Tower now known as the Queen's House, heartbroken and alone. There are many reports of her ghost returning to haunt the room. Somewhat ungallantly, Seymour subsequently returned to England, became an MP and remarried, making something of a mockery of Arabella's love, loyalty and unswerving devotion.

OVERBURY'S INADVERTENT OVERDOSE
1613

Plenty of people have breathed their last at the Tower of London over the years. The majority shuffled off this mortal coil after a good old-fashioned beheading, a no-nonsense hanging or a straight-forward firing squad. You used to know where you were at the Tower when it came to executions.

That all changed in September 1613 when the noted poet and essayist Sir Thomas Overbury mysteriously kicked the bucket while in custody at the Tower and a story so labyrinthine it makes the plot of *Game Of Thrones* look simplistic began to emerge. We're talking politics, greed, infidelity, the King and a jam tart laced with sulphuric acid here, so strap yourself in.

It is 1604 and a young but penniless Overbury heads to London with his best friend Robert Carr. The duo do very well for themselves in the Big Smoke and by 1612 Overbury has already been knighted and Carr has become King James I's *de facto* right-hand man. Life is good.

Trouble of course is just over the horizon and, not for the first time, it's woman shaped. Carr begins an affair with the married Frances Howard, the Countess of Essex, and at roughly the same time Overbury publishes a poem entitled *The Wife* in which he extols the virtues a man should look for in a woman before popping down to Ernest Jones and buying the ring.

Unsurprisingly Lady Essex interprets the poem as a bit of a dig at her. Overbury and her powerful family, the Howards, have already got previous and she vows to put him in his place, whispering a few choice words in the King's ears and before you can say 'hell hath no fury like a woman scorned (or insulted)', he's thrown into the

Tower. It's not an executable offence but a bit of porridge should shut him up. It certainly did and on 14 September, Overbury bought the farm.

Nothing initially seemed untoward but two years after his death, the Governor of the Tower wrote to James to tell him he had since learned one of the guards had been plying Overbury with 'poisoned food and medicine' during his incarceration and the royal court was suddenly awash with rumours about who had got to him and why. The King's name was even mentioned (albeit very quietly) and in the end James had no choice but to authorise a trial.

It was a humdinger. The judges were Edward Coke and Sir Francis Bacon (yes, that one). What they uncovered would have kept a modern tabloid newspaper in business for months.

Carr wanted Overbury out of the way. With James' royal approval, Lady Essex was getting her marriage annulled (her husband was allegedly impotent) so she could tie the knot with Carr and he knew his old mate, a fierce opponent of both remarrying and the Howard family, would definitely make a scene at the wedding.

The Tower was the perfect place to keep him out of the way but Lady Essex was determined 'he should return no more to this stage' and devised a more permanent solution, getting the incumbent Lord Lieutenant of the Tower replaced with 'her man', and a chap named Robert Weston who was by all accounts 'well acquainted with the power of drugs', was appointed Overbury's jailer.

The rest was easy. Overbury was unwittingly fed a subtle diet of sulphuric acid in the form of copper vitriol that was hidden in his tarts and jellies and before long he was sleeping with the fishes.

Lady Essex admitted her guilt at the trial but although Carr refused to put his hands up, both were convicted and sentenced to death. They were eventually pardoned but four of their accomplices, including Weston, were hanged.

THE ARMOURIES'
GEOGRAPHICAL
GAFFE
1614

Museums are cathedrals of information, the depositories of centuries of national culture, learning and collective consciousness. The worldwide web is all well and good but museums are the undisputed kings of scholarly pursuit.

They do, however, sometimes tell us porkies. They don't mean to but with thousands of exhibits, artefacts and historical documents to contend with, it's inevitable they're going to drop the ball from time to time. Even normally unflappable curators have their bad days and so it was in the 17th century when a fetching suit of Japanese armour went on display at the Royal Armouries at the Tower of London.

The armour had been a present from the Shogun, Tokugawa Hidetada. He had given it to John Saris of the East India Company while he was on a trade visit as a gift for James I and Saris dutifully handed it over to his King on his return to London in 1614.

What happened to the Shogun's generous gift for the next 30 years or so is a mystery but in 1650 there is mention in the King's sale inventory of 'armor, a head piece, a vizard, back and brest, two sleeves with gantlets, one placard for ye breast and for ye back, two pieces for ye thighs and legs and three small breast plates.'

By the early 1660s the exotic, Japanese armour was on display and attracting big crowds. 'Many persons of quality went to the armoury in the Tower of London,' recorded Thomas Rugge in his contemporary journal *Mercurius Politicus Redivivus*, 'to see that most notable and strong defence for the body, the suit of armour sent from the emperor Mogul, which suit was presented to His Majesty the King Of England.'

The problem is that the 'emperor Mogul' in 17th century England was understood to be the ruler of India and not Japan. Rugge was merely echoing the mistake in the Armouries' own labelling, meaning the scores of visitors who came to gaze at the armour left under the false impression it was Indian rather than Japanese. Quite a geographical clanger but it was, after all, in an era before Google Maps.

The suit of armour is still on display in the Royal Armouries museum but did make a temporary return home to Japan in 1972 after it had fallen into disrepair and had to be restored by the master armourer Hiromichi Miura.

KEEPING UP WITH
THE JONESES
1619

The Banqueting House in Whitehall is the hidden gem of the collection of Royal Palaces and although it may not have witnessed as many momentous events or as much political upheaval as its more famous cousins in the capital, it nonetheless boasts a rich and fascinating history.

Its first surprising secret is it is not even the original Banqueting House. The first was built in 1581 in the reign of Elizabeth I but it was a wood and canvas prefab affair that did not age well and early in the 17th century James I commissioned a new, sturdier construction for his entertaining and general royal merriment.

Unfortunately, he absolutely hated the end result, complaining his new building lacked space and light, but his regal disappointment lasted just two short years when, in 1619, the second Banqueting House burned down after careless household staff set light to the place, 'accidentally' igniting some of the scenery which had been installed for one of the Royal Masques (more of which shortly). The insurance company had their suspicions but they couldn't prove a thing.

James, of course, feigned horror but even before the last embers had been extinguished, he summoned his Surveyor of the King's Works, Inigo Jones, to draw up plans for the third incarnation of the Banqueting House, the one that still stands in central London today.

Jones' design envisaged a building in the classic Roman style he had seen during his travels through Italy, a double cubed construction measuring nearly 34m (111½ft) long, 17m (56ft) wide and almost 17m (56ft) in height. He estimated the cost at £9,850 and although the final bill was double the figure, James was mercifully delighted with his new pad, which dominated the otherwise ramshackle skyline around Whitehall.

So what of the Royal Masques? A shortlived trend popularised by James and his wife Queen Anne, a masque was essentially an extravagant party-cum-theatrical performance which the guests and actors alike attended in fancy dress. There was poetry, there was music, there was dancing and, most significantly, there was also moving scenery and dramatic, scripted scenes.

Which is where Mr Jones resurfaces in our story. A carpenter by trade who graduated to become an architectural advisor to the Court and the man behind Banqueting House, he was also responsible for devising the lavish the scenery for the Royal Masques and in a long-term collaboration with the celebrated writer Ben Johnson, he helped stage over 500 performances between 1605 and 1640.

The two men enjoyed a fraught working relationship. Jones insisted his props were the beating heart of the masque while Johnson argued the words he supplied for the actors were the real crowd pleaser.

It was probably only their mutual fear of displeasing the monarch that kept the pair together although Johnson did find a way of venting his frustration, ridiculing Jones in his works such as *The Masque Of Augurs, Bartholomew Fair* and *Love's Welcome At Bolsover* with a series of unlikeable characters based on his partner.

The popularity of masques however waned relatively quickly and by 1740 the whole expensive business was dead. As were both Jones and Johnson, who never did reconcile their artistic differences.

DEN OF ROYAL INIQUITY
1622

When you think of the Royal Palaces, it is hard not to conjure up images of regal splendour, priceless works of art, peerless architecture and a general sense of elegance and opulence in equal measure. The British monarchy have certainly enjoyed the domestic perks of the job over the years.

But even kings and queens like to relax and kick back and when James I commissioned Inigo Jones to build the Banqueting House, he had one very specific request. The King wanted a room in which he and his friends could have a few drinks, make merry and generally have a bit of a knees-up away from the prying eyes of the Royal Court and pious disapproval.

Jones came up with 'The Undercroft' at Banqueting House, the very epitome of a private drinking den for only the most exclusive of guests. Situated under the main hall, The Undercroft was a brick-lined, vaulted pleasure dome par excellence where the King 'did regale himself privately' and everyone had a thoroughly good time.

The Undercroft quickly earned a reputation as the place to be for high-end drinkies and a year after Banqueting House was completed in 1622, Ben Johnson wrote a dedication to the place, cementing its reputation as the number one party location in royal circles. It read:

> Since Bacchus, thou art father
> Of wines, to thee the rather
> We dedicate this Cellar
> Where now, thou art made Dweller.

After James' death in 1625, however, The Undercroft became something of an unofficial casino as well as a drinking den and in

1664 the diarist John Evelyn recorded a royal gambling spree below Banqueting House in which 'the King [Charles II], Queen-Consort and Queen Mother' won only 'a trifle'. They should, of course, have put it all on black rather than red.

As the Banqueting House fell out of royal favour, The Undercroft mended its occasionally debauched ways and is now available for hire by the great unwashed masses for parties, receptions and drinks. Which is, after all, essentially where this particular palatial story started.

A DIPLOMATIC FAUX PAS
1626

As the more attentive of you will hopefully remember, the Banqueting House initially served as the setting for a series of lavish and exorbitantly expensive 'masques' (see Keeping Up With The Joneses, page 39) but it was also a place where important matters of state were attended to, most notably regularly hosting receptions for visiting foreign diplomats and dignitaries.

According to the strict protocol, the diplomats would arrive at the north entrance of Banqueting House while the king would enter the building via the south entrance, plonking his royal derrière on the chair of state positioned under the throne canopy in readiness to greet his latest important visitor.

With the monarch comfortably seated, the diplomat would be guided by the Lord Chamberlain and the Master of Ceremonies into the great hall and a carefully choreographed show would begin. Not quite as carefully choreographed as a photo shoot of David Cameron relaxing on holiday in Cornwall *en famille*, perhaps, but finely tuned nonetheless.

The diplomat was expected to take two steps and bow, which the King acknowledged by rising from his chair. The visitor would then proceed to the middle of the hall and bow again and the king would remove his hat. When the dignitary finally reached the dais on which the king was standing, he would make a third and final bow. The intricate ritual was completed when the monarch invited the diplomat to join him on the dais and present his credentials.

The system usually worked jolly well but occasionally the complex instructions issued to the visiting representatives were lost in translation and according to contemporary reports from 1626, the Persian diplomat made a right royal dog's dinner of his public show of respect to King Charles I.

'Entering the banqueting house where his Majesty stood under the state canopy to receive him, he advanced without one look or gesture of respect till, coming close to the king's person, he clapped his letters to his eyes one after the other, kissed them and pressed them into the hands of his Majesty, but not so much as bowing his body at their delivery.

'Having thus finished this little ceremony, he in his retreat after some twenty paces made with his back to the king turned about and, waving his hand on each side, imperiously as commanding a prospect hindered by the multitude that pressed in between his sight and the king's, he made a kind of stooping reverence then a second and a third, and departed.'

Charles was not amused and the diplomat was so abashed when his mistake was pointed out that he promised to bring a selection of fine rugs on his next visit as way of apology.

A SUPERSTITIOUS START
1631

It was back in 1781 that King George III splashed out the then princely sum of £20,000 to add Kew Palace to the Royal Family's bulging property portfolio but the grand old house was originally built in 1631 by a Samuel Fortrey, a wealthy silk merchant who yearned for a country retreat and weekends away from the hustle and bustle of central London.

Construction of the building was a huge undertaking, involving hundreds of craftsmen without a JCB, orbital sander or cement mixer between them and it took months for the big house to rise solemnly upwards from its foundations. An awful lot of tea and biscuits were consumed in the process.

The work however would have been significantly quicker had it not been for the 17th century carpenters responsible for installing the massive oak beams required to support the roof of the new house.

The problem was our carpenters, like many of their contemporaries, were a superstitious mob and it was a widely held belief that evil spirits and witches were floating all about the place, patiently waiting for their first chance to transform into cats or frogs and cast mischievous spells on the unsuspecting, sleeping residents of a house.

To counter this perceived supernatural threat, the carpenters wasted precious time carving 'witch-marks' into the timbers to combat the ethereal menace, gouging out the symbols near windows, doors and fireplaces and any other points in the house that were deemed vulnerable.

The marks – a circle with four, opposing diagonal lines protruding from the bottom – were discovered in the roof spaces at Kew in 2004, enduring evidence that the workmen were more concerned with ghosts than finishing on time.

'Most of the archaeological evidence in old houses is very practical,' explained Kew Palace curator Lee Prosser. 'But here we have something purely superstitious. It gives us a tantalising glimpse into the fears and concerns of our ancestors.'

Carvings, however, were not the only contemporary measure considered effective in scaring off the dark side. 'Urine bottles' filled with hair and nail clippings were often hidden in secret cavities during a new build while old shoes, mummified cats and kittens would frequently be hidden under the floorboards to discourage any unwelcome ghoulish invasion. The RSPCA were firm advocates of the old-shoe method.

MADE TO MEASURE
1636

When the initial euphoria of moving into a new home subsides, the new owner is inevitably faced with the thorny question of decorating. Almond White or Mellow Mocha in the living room? Tangerine Twist or Moroccan Flame for the kitchen? The options are exhaustingly endless.

King Charles I faced a similar, albeit grander dilemma in the early 1630s as he contemplated embellishing the ceiling of Banqueting House. The roof space was embarrassingly bare and the King urgently needed something to jazz the place up a bit.

There were no shortage of eager artists desperate for such a high-profile commission but Charles eventually turned to Peter Paul Rubens, the celebrated Flemish diplomat-cum-artist, to do the job and after making a preliminary sketch (which is now on show at Tate Britain for the culture vultures among you) of his vision for the ceiling, it was agreed he would produce nine painted canvas panels for the Banqueting House. Rubens retired to his workshop in Antwerp to begin the project and by the summer of 1634, the work was finished.

The first hitch however came after the completed panels were left in the corner of the workshop. When they were unfurled 'having been rolled up almost a year', cracks were discovered in the paint and Rubens and his team had to embark on a rapid repair job.

In early 1636 the restored canvases finally arrived in London but when they were once again unfurled, it emerged some of the panels were too big for their allotted spaces while others were not large enough. A schoolboy error indeed, which prompted some last-minute alterations to extend some of the panels and trim others until finally the beautiful canvases could be installed in their new setting.

Rubens was paid £3,000 for his endeavours, plus a gold chain in lieu of a bonus, and we can only hope he invested some of the money on a tape measure.

To be fair to Rubens what he may have lacked in accuracy, he more than made up for with artistic talent and the nine panels – the centrepiece of which is entitled *The Apotheosis of James I* – are a stunning piece of work which visitors to Banqueting House can still enjoy if they are prepared to crane their necks.

CHARLES' CANINE BETRAYAL
1647

As we have already learned, even the Tower of London doesn't boast a 100 per cent record when it comes to what is now euphemistically referred to as 'successful prisoner retention' (see Flambard's Double First, page 14) but the Tower was actually a penal bastion in comparison to Hampton Court when it was pressed into service as a jail.

This was good news for Charles I when he found himself incarcerated at Hampton by Oliver Cromwell and his ghastly Parliamentarians in 1647 towards the end of the English Civil War. The regime by the banks of the Thames was decidedly relaxed and it wasn't long before the King decided he'd had enough of being caged.

In truth, his imprisonment was not exactly a hardship. Charles was permitted his own servants and billeted in a suite of sumptuous rooms overlooking the Privy Garden. He was even permitted to play tennis on the palace's indoor court but he remained desperate to escape and get on with the pressing business of losing the throne.

A cunning plan was not required. On the 11 November, his chief jailor Colonel Edward Whalley arrived at the King's bedchamber at five o'clock sharp to escort Charles to the chapel at Hampton but was told the monarch was busy writing letters. Whalley returned at six to be rebuffed again and by seven o'clock, he smelled a rat and forced his way into the bedroom via the Privy Stairs at the back of the King's suite.

To Whalley's chagrin, Charles had of course legged it, jumping on a boat waiting on the river, and sailed off to the Isle of Wight. The royal escapee already had a five-hour head start on his incompetent captors.

But Charles' chronological advantage could have been significantly greater had it not been for the disloyalty of his pet dog.

'This day will be famous in aftertimes because towards the end of it his Majesty escaped a kind of restraint under which he was at Hampton Court,' reported the contemporary newsletter *Moderate Intelligencer*.

'According to the best relation, thus: he, as was usuall, went to be private a little before evening prayer; staying somewhat longer then usuall, it was taken notice of, yet at first without suspition; but he not coming forth, suddenly there were fears, which increased by the crying of a greyhound again and again within, and upon search it was found the king was gone.'

So much for dogs being a man's best friend.

To be fair, Charles still managed to make his way to the Isle of Wight despite his mutt's inopportune moaning but it ultimately proved to be a Pyrrhic success.

The King threw himself on the mercy of the island's Parliamentary Governor, Colonel Robert Hammond who, he believed, was privately something of a royal sympathiser. He miscalculated and Hammond threw Charles back in jail in Carisbrook Castle (which didn't quite boast the same sporting facilities as Hampton Court) and promptly informed Cromwell he had apprehended the AWOL monarch.

THE ANONYMOUS
EXECUTIONER
1649

As we discovered in Den Of Royal Iniquity (see page 41), Charles I enjoyed some high times inside Banqueting House but it was just outside the walls of the royal residence that the ill-fated King met his maker in 1649 when he was beheaded on the orders of Parliament.

Poor old Charlie was sentenced to death after being indicted by the Rump Parliament. One of the charges was that he was responsible for the estimated 300,000 deaths on both sides during the English Civil War, which rather neglected the fact it takes two to tango, but Charles knew the game was up and refused to enter any sort of plea.

His fate sealed, the deposed monarch was led from his temporary prison at St James' Palace on the morning of 30 January, through the rooms of Banqueting House he knew so well and outside onto a specially constructed scaffold to face the music. It was a typically cold winter's day and Charles wore two shirts to ensure he did not shiver lest the assembled crowd assume he was trembling with fear. A quick glass of red wine also helped to keep the chill out and steady the nerves.

'You hasten to a crown of glory,' Doctor Juxon, the Bishop of London, glibly announced. 'I go from a corruptible to an incorruptible crown,' Charles famously replied, 'where no disturbance can be.' The executioner swung with great accuracy, decapitating Charlie in one fell swoop, and England's first state-endorsed case of regicide was complete.

So far a well-worn story but the twist is the identity of the mercifully adept axe man. Or more accurately, no-one is sure exactly who the hell he was.

On the morning of the King's execution, the regular executioner was nowhere to be found. Perhaps he had secret royalist sympathies. Perhaps he didn't want the inevitable infamy that would come with lopping off Charles' head. Perhaps he had a doctor's appointment.

The immediate result of the mysterious disappearance was the urgent need to find a replacement. One was evidently located but as the executioner was masked with a pantomime villain's hood, we remain in the dark about his true identity.

We do know the official Hangman of London, one Richard Brandon, was approached but he said rope rather than axes were his thing. An Irishman by the name of Gunning is put forward by some as the man with the chopper but while there is a plaque in Galway naming him as the executioner, the evidence is circumstantial. Captain William Hewlett, the senior army office on the fateful day, was retrospectively convicted of regicide in 1660 following the Restoration of the Monarchy but the phrase 'convenient scapegoat' springs alarmingly to mind while there are numerous other spurious myths about the name of the elusive axe man.

It's likely we will now never know. What is beyond doubt is Charles lost his head and the monarchy never quite recovered its former, omnipotent glories ever again.

ALL THAT GLITTERS IS NOT (SOLID) GOLD

1660

Truth is the first casualty of war, closely followed by the poor bloody soldiers on the frontline. The English Civil War between 1642 and 1651 claimed an estimated 300,000 lives and the Crown Jewels, seemingly safely housed in the Tower of London, took one hell of a battering as well.

King Charles I was clearly a careless monarch and lost control of the Tower to Oliver Cromwell and the Roundheads early in the conflict and the rebels suddenly had unfettered access to a treasure trove of really rather expensive jewellery.

In 1643 leading Parliamentarian Henry Marten – who was later to be one of the 59 signatories on Charles' death warrant – let himself into the vaults and forced open the chest he found there. He removed the assorted crowns and sceptres and indulged in a sarcastic game of dressing up. 'Being crowned and royally arrayed, he did march about the room with a stately garb,' relates *A Chronicle of the Coronations of the Queens Regnant of England*, published in 1838. 'And afterwards with a thousand apish and ridiculous actions, exposed those sacred ornaments to contempt and laughter.'

Much, much worse was to follow. The sparkling symbols of royal power and privilege had to go permanently and less than a week after Charles suffered the dreaded chop, Parliament ordered the collection 'to be totally broken and that they melt down all the gold and silver and sell the jewels to the best advantage of the Commonwealth.'

The vultures circled as, bit by bit, the collection was exchanged for hard cash. The Tudor State Crown – set with 28 diamonds, 19 sapphires, 37 rubies and 168 pearls – was valued at £1,100 (or £1.74 million in today's money) and the Crown Jewels were dispersed.

In 1660, however, the tide turned with the restoration of the monarchy and the newly-crowned Charles II decided any king worth his salt really ought to have lots of lovely shiny things, so he ordered Sir Robert Vyner, the royal goldsmith, to undo the destruction wreaked by that cad Cromwell.

He had a job on his hands. Much of the gold settings for the various diamonds and gemstones in the collection had been melted down for coins. Charles simply could not afford to replace like for like and Vyner was forced to order a truly staggering three tons of cheaper silver to restock the King's Jewel House.

Which is why not all that glitters is actually solid gold (we got there eventually), with many of the current Crown Jewels predominantly silver with the fig leaf of a gold leaf façade.

THE GREAT UNWASHED
1660

Banqueting House may have enjoyed a relatively short stint as a royal palace but although it may have lacked in terms of longevity it was nonetheless the scene of sumptuous state occasions, some cracking parties and, lest we forget, the infamous beheading of Charles I (see The Anonymous Executioner, page 51).

However, one of the most surprising ceremonies conducted inside the walls of the grand old building must surely have been the Royal Maundy, the annual tradition of the monarch distributing money and gifts to the poor on the Thursday before Easter Sunday.

The tradition dates back to King John in the 13th century and, after briefly falling out of favour, it was restored in 1660 when Charles II became King. The local poor were over the moon.

Banqueting House was frequently although not exclusively used as the backdrop for the public show of royal largesse and it was certainly a profitable gig if you were chosen to receive a handout, as a contemporary account of the 1774 service testifies.

'His Majesty's alms were distributed to thirty-five poor men and women, three ells of Holland, a piece of woollen cloth, a pair of shoes and stockings, 20 shillings in a purse, 35 silver pence, a loaf of bread and a platter of fish to each.'

Nothing particularly unusual in that you may think but another integral part of Royal Maundy was the act of pedilavium, the ritual of the reigning monarch washing the feet of the aforementioned poor and, let's face it, it's not every day you witness a king or queen giving a tramp a soapy pedicure.

The tradition evokes the story of Jesus washing the feet of his disciples in the Bible. Monarchs with a penchant for good PR were eager to portray themselves in the same 'servant king' light as the fella with the beard and the act of pedilavium was born.

The problem, of course, was that the poor in those days were not exactly paragons of personal hygiene. The monarch may have wanted to appear publicly as a thoroughly down-to-earth egg but putting their hands on filthy feet was off the menu.

The solution was a clandestine clean-up before the odorous peasant got anywhere near the boss. A servant would give the feet a preliminary scrub before court officials undertook two further washes and only then would they be allowed to go before the monarch for their bizarre bath. Even then the water was heavily scented with perfume lest any unpleasant smells lingered.

Charles II and his successor James II both tickled the tootsies at Banqueting House but the last record of a monarch personally fondling feet is William III in 1698. The Royal Maundy tradition of gifting money survives to this day although Queen Elizabeth is doubtless delighted the pedilavium aspect of the ceremony has long since been consigned to history.

THE FIFTH CUT IS THE DEEPEST
1685

According to Rod Stewart, the first cut is the deepest but that sadly proved to be a forlorn hope for James Scott, the first Duke of Monmouth, when his head was forcibly separated from his body in the shadow of the Tower of London.

Monmouth was the eldest but illegitimate son of Charles II and after a successful military career during the third Anglo-Dutch War in the 1670s, he set his sights a little higher and decided to lead a Protestant uprising against his uncle, King James II, in an attempt to seize the throne.

The 'Monmouth Rebellion' was not a big hit. In fact, it was about as successful as Sir Clive Sinclair's attempts to break the monopoly of the motor car and after his forces were routed by the King's troops at the Battle of Sedgemoor, Monmouth was hauled off to prison and sentenced to death.

Which is where his troubles really started. On 15 July 1685, he was dragged onto Tower Hill and delivered into the hands of the axe man Jack Ketch, who proved to be the last man on earth you'd want swinging away in an inexpert and bloody effort to send you off to your maker.

'The first blow inflicted only a slight wound,' wrote Lord Macaulay in his book *The History of England*.

'The Duke struggled, rose from the block and looked reproachfully at the executioner. The head sank down once more. The stroke was repeated again and again but still the neck was not severed and the body continued to move.

'Yells of rage and horror rose from the crowd. Ketch flung down the axe with a curse. 'I cannot do it,' he said, 'my heart fails me.' 'Take up the axe, man,' cried the sheriff. 'Fling him over the rails,' roared the mob. At length the axe was taken up. Two more blows extinguished the last remains of life but a knife was used to separate the head from the shoulders.

'The crowd was wrought up to such an ecstasy of rage that the executioner was in danger of being torn in pieces and was conveyed away under a strong guard.'

Some historians claim it actually took seven or even eight blows rather than Macaulay's five to successfully finish off the poor Monmouth but whatever the final figure, it was an undeniably brutal and painful way to go.

The doomed Duke's story may have ended here but legend has it that one further indignity lay in store for Monmouth when it was realised after his execution that he had never sat for an official portrait and traitor or not, it was not proper for a person with royal (albeit illegitimate) blood to pass without the attentions of an artist. And so, the legend goes, his body was quickly exhumed and dressed in fine attire, his head stitched back on and the Duke was finally immortalised in paint.

A tale that would no doubt make Stephen King purr but somewhat undermined by the fact there are at least two depictions of Monmouth still hanging in the National Portrait Gallery which predate his messy execution.

THE ARTIST TURNED AGRICULTURIST

1685

The famed French impressionist Claude Monet once observed that 'my garden is my most beautiful masterpiece' and for many of those with naturally green fingers and lashings of spare time and patience, horticulture is indeed an art form.

There's no pictorial evidence to back up Monet's bold claims about his gardening talents but one celebrated artist who was undeniably handy with the secateurs was Italian Antonio Verrio, a man who extensively decorated Hampton Court Palace but also found time to knock the gardens at St James's Park into shape.

Verrio arrived in Britain in 1672 and on the recommendation of Ralph Montagu, the English Ambassador in Paris, was commissioned by Charles II to decorate the North Range of Windsor Castle, collaborating with the architect Hugh May and sculptor Grinling Gibbons on the project. The King was reportedly 'well satisfied' with his work in the Baroque mural style on the Windsor's ceilings, staircases, chapel and St George's Hall and Verrio was consequently appointed his 'Chief and First Painter'.

Charles' death in 1685 saw the Italian's career take a surprising turn and in March that year he became 'Keeper of the Great Garden in St James's Park' on a generous annual salary of 400 pounds. It seemed Verrio had traded in his paintbrushes for the trowel and potting shed on a permanent basis.

According to contemporary reports, he transformed the garden into a 'very delicious paradise' but his stint at St James's was not without incident as he became embroiled in a feud with a Lady Williams, who complained bitterly that his alterations to a greenhouse were playing havoc with the tomatoes in her garden.

Verrio's artistic exploits were still not yet over. The ascension of William III to the throne in 1689 changed the landscape and although the staunch Catholic initially refused to work for the new Protestant King, he returned to royal service in 1699, dusted off his paints and began work at Hampton Court.

The palace's King's Staircase, the Great Bedchamber, the Banqueting House, the King's Little Bedchamber and the Queen's Drawing Room all received Verrio's distinctive Baroque treatment and despite his sabbatical at St James', he had not lost his touch.

His work in the Banqueting House and his depiction of naked nymphs was certainly risqué and some years later an unnamed resident at Hampton Court requested his work be painted over in the name of decency. Thankfully, prudence triumphed over prudism, large pieces of furniture were strategically moved to obscure the offending images and Verrio's work survived.

Sadly, Verrio's eyesight failed him late in life and in his enforced retirement he was granted an annual pension of £200 and lodgings at Hampton Court by Queen Anne. Verrio died in June 1707, the end of an accomplished career in which he made an inedible mark both on canvas and on the great outdoors.

BEASTLY FATALITY
AT THE TOWER
1686

Zoos have a tendency to divide public opinion. For some they are an exploitative monstrosity, a symbol of man's casual cruelty to his cousins in the animal kingdom and an institution that should have long since been consigned to the dustbin of history. Others just can't get enough of the overpriced toy pandas in the gift shop.

Critics of the whole zoo concept would have certainly been appalled by the exotic assortment of beasts housed at the Tower of London over the centuries. Not quite as appalled those who are forced to fork out nearly £100 for a family of four for London Zoo today but jolly angry nonetheless.

The Royal Menagerie began back in 1235 when the Holy Roman Emperor Frederick II found the answer to the age old question of 'what do you buy a man who has everything?' and presented King Henry III with three lions as a gift. A few years later King Haakon of Norway jumped on the bandwagon and gave Henry a polar bear and before anyone could even question the morality of keeping wild animals in captivity, the Tower was knee deep in leopards, hyenas, elephants and inebriated zebras (more of which later).

The tradition of keeping animals at the Tower persisted but there are, of course, inherent dangers in housing disgruntled 270kg (600lb) predators in your back garden and in 1686 a young woman by the name of Mary Jenkinson paid the ultimate price for the folly when she was mauled by a lion.

Mary was the other half of the Tower's keeper of the lions when one of the big cats caught her arm 'with his claws and mouth and most miserably tore her flesh from the bone.' Surgeons amputated the arm but Mary did not survive the experience.

A century later tragedy almost struck the Tower again but this time it was the resident monkeys rather than the lions who were the culprits, attacking a young visitor. 'Formerly several monkies [sic] were kept,' read an early 19th century guidebook, 'but one of them having torn a boy's leg in a dangerous manner they were removed.'

Further, more minor attacks by various ill-disciplined animals followed and in 1835 the Duke of Wellington, who was topping up his pension as the Constable of the Tower, decided all the monkey business had gone far enough and the Royal Menagerie was finally closed and the majority of the animals transferred to Regents Park, hastening the birth of the modern London Zoo.

And the intoxicated zebra? According to legend, the native of Africa would happily wander around the gardens within the Tower and even allowed a boy to ride her but her favourite pastime was sneaking into the soldiers' canteen and helping herself to beer. A black and white case of theft if ever there was one.

WHEN THE WIND BLOWS
1688

The British obsession with the vagaries of the weather is as tedious as it well documented but the golden weather vane that sits proudly at the north end of the roof of the Banqueting House owes its existence to military rather than meteorological matters.

Workmen were despatched to the roof to install the imposing wrought-iron vane in the autumn of 1688. The country was in the grip of a political and religious crisis and James II wanted to know, both literally and metaphorically, which way the wind was blowing.

The King was in serious trouble. Crowned in 1685, James' attempts to create controversial religious freedom for England's Catholic minority had earned him powerful enemies and in June 1688 seven leading Protestant nobles invited William, the Protestant Prince of Orange, to nip over the Channel with an army, oust James and put a stop to all his ecumenical nonsense.

William was jolly keen on the idea and by September his army was ready to sail. All that he required was a favourable wind to get his fleet to English soil and the county waited apprehensively for the hostilities to commence.

James was understandably eager not to be caught with his pants down and ordered the weather vane at Banqueting House put in place. As long as the wind came from the west, William would be confined to port and the King was safe.

His luck held for three months but in early November the arrow on the weather vane gave an ominous creak as it swung around in the opposite direction. A 'Protestant wind' from the east was now blowing and after stocking up with Duty Free, William and his army were finally on their way.

They landed at Brixham in Devon on 5 November. Despite enjoying a numerical advantage, James' forces melted away faster than a Cornetto in a microwave and in December the King decided cowardice was the better part of valour and tried to flee to France. He was captured and imprisoned but William wasn't into regicide and quietly allowed James to escape to the sanctuary of the court of King Louis XIV of France, James' cousin and ally.

Two years later James attempted to recapture the throne by raising an army in Ireland but he was knocked out in the third round by William at the Battle of the Boyne and the last Catholic King of England returned to France to live out the rest of his life in exile.

Banqueting House's part in the story is not yet over. In February 1689 William and his wife Mary were jointly offered the crown in the building, just metres below the weather vane that James had, ahem, vainly hoped would be his salvation.

MARY'S NEAR MISS
1689

Queen Mary II spent a fleeting five years as Britain's first constitutional monarch in tandem with her husband William III before smallpox claimed her life but had it not been for a fortuitous twist of fate, Mary's reign may have been significantly shorter.

William and Mary were crowned in April 1689 and while her husband quickly packed the royal suitcase and headed off to Ireland to wage war against the Jacobites, the new queen focused on the couple's domestic arrangements.

The problem was neither of the new monarchs were particularly enamoured with the idea of living at Whitehall Palace. The damp pad down by the Thames played hell with William's asthma and Mary couldn't abide the curtains.

A new home was urgently required and the royal couple fell in love with a Jacobean mansion by the name of Nottingham House in Kensington which was owned by William's Secretary of State, Daniel Finch, the Earl of Nottingham. The location was said to have 'a very good air' and after the wheezy King and his Queen popped down the Post Office to withdraw £20,000 to meet Finch's asking price, the history of Kensington Palace as a royal residence began.

But like all couples, William and Mary wanted to put their own mark on the new place and Mary politely but firmly ordered Sir Christopher Wren, Surveyor of the King's Work, to get cracking on giving the palace a serious makeover. The builders descended and the hammering, sawing, incessant tea breaks and wolf whistling began in earnest.

Mary, however, was not the most patient of clients, visiting the site almost daily to 'hasten the workmen'. She was desperate to move in and have the girls around for a gossip, so to meet her exacting timetable, shortcuts were taken as vaults were built on bad foundations and walls raised before the lime mortar had enough time to dry and settle.

In November 1689 Mary very nearly paid the ultimate price for her impatience when a section of the new building collapsed, sending scaffolding, timber and masonry crashing to the floor and killing one unfortunate builder in the process. The Queen had been on site only minutes before the fatal accident.

'It pleased God to show me the uncertainties of things,' she wrote in a letter to William after her narrow escape. 'For part of the house which was new built fell down. It shewed me the hand of God plainly in it and I was truly humbled.'

Humbled perhaps but mercifully unscathed and despite the setback, William and Mary moved into Kensington Palace on Christmas Eve 1689.

That, though, is not the end of the palace's early troubles and two years later a fire started in the Great Court. This time there were no deaths but the blaze was only brought under control when the servants dashed to the cellar and used the beer bottles they found there to douse the flames.

A terrible waste of good beer perhaps but a welcome reprieve for the latest royal residence.

MARY'S ELUSIVE SCEPTRE
1689

We all mislay things from time to time. Car keys love nothing more than jumping down the back of the sofa, mobile phones take an almost sadistic relish in disappearing into the deepest recesses of the kitchen drawer and wallets think it's absolutely hilarious to hide themselves in the jeans you're about to put on a hot wash.

Trivial misplacements, however, in comparison to the very careless case of storage that was uncovered at the Tower of London in the 19th century when Queen Mary II's glittering Sceptre with Dove went missing for half a century.

The golden, jewel-encrusted staff was specially commissioned for Mary's joint coronation with hubby William at Westminster Abbey in April 1689. The sceptre did a sterling job of looking regal and rather expensive but as soon as the ceremony was over, it was taken back to the Tower to meet all the other Crown Jewels.

It was never used again and in the early 1760s, an absent-minded member of staff popped it at the back of a cupboard and neglected to tell anyone. Everyone forgot about the poor sceptre and it was not until 1814 that it was accidentally unearthed when they were having a bit of a spring clean in the Tower.

'I take this opportunity of mentioning another [part of the Crown Jewels] which was discovered in the year 1814 at the Jewel Office in the Tower of London,' wrote Arthur Taylor in his book *The Glory of Regality: An Historical Treatise of the Anointing and Crowning of the Kings and Queens of England*, published just six years after the bizarre discovery.

> '[It was] lying at the back part of a shelf and enveloped in dust. It was found to be a rod of gold with its emblem, the dove, resting on a cross like that of the king. It is of elegant

workmanship and is adorned with coloured gems. No account has been given to the public of this neglected ensign of regality but it may be conjectured to have been made for the consort of William III.'

The Brasso was quickly cracked open to give the AWOL rod a much-needed buff up and the sceptre was finally returned to the Crown Jewels with strict instructions to stay in sight at all times.

WHITEHALL SUCCUMBS
TO THE FLAMES
1698

In its 17th century pomp, the Banqueting House was the centrepiece of a far larger royal complex of the Palace of Whitehall, a sprawling collection of buildings near the banks of the Thames that was said to boast more than 1500 rooms in total and was bigger than either the Vatican or the Palace of Versailles.

Today Banqueting House is bereft of its former regal neighbours and it remains something of a miracle the building still survives given the ferocious fire that raged around its elegant walls in 1698, the devastating result of a lackadaisical servant who failed to follow orders.

The blaze broke out on 4 January after a Dutch maidservant left laundry to dry by a charcoal brazier. Palace rules strictly forbade such a potentially disastrous act and sure enough the clothes caught fire and the flames rapidly fanned out, inexorably engulfing the assorted wooden structures that compromised Whitehall.

Unfortunately there was no contemporary equivalent of Red Adair on hand to douse the flames, the fire fighters who did attend the blaze were severely hampered by servants scampering around under orders to save royal works of art and the pumps deployed to supply the water were woefully underpowered.

The fire burned for 15 long hours before it was finally brought under control but almost as soon as the last flame was extinguished, it suddenly reignited. Banqueting House had survived the initial fiery onslaught but the second fire renewed the danger and William II ordered the south window of the building to be bricked up to protect the interior.

The King's emergency measure and Banqueting House's stone walls saved the day and along with the Whitehall and Holbein gates, it lived to fight another day. Conflicting reports put the number of fatalities at anywhere between 12 and 30 but rumours of Whitehall's demise were not exaggerated.

'It is a dismal sight to behold,' bemoaned a witness to the destruction, 'such a glorious, famous and much renowned palace reduced to rubbish and ashes, which the day before might justly contend with any palace in the world for riches, nobility, honour and grandeur.'

A new Palace of Whitehall never did rise from the ashes. Four days after the blaze Sir Christopher Wren was ordered to convert Banqueting House into a royal chapel to deputise for the Tudor Chapel that had been razed to the ground in the fire but William was already happily housed at Kensington Palace and there was simply no will to restore Whitehall to its former glories.

A new London grew up around Banqueting House in the subsequent years while the careless maidservant was promptly given her P45.

PETER THE PARTY ANIMAL
1698

They say a picture paints a thousand words but in the case of the elegant and tasteful portrait of Peter the Great, Tsar of Russia, which today hangs on the south wall of the Queen's Gallery at Kensington Palace, nothing could be further from the truth.

The picture was painted during Peter's visit to Britain back in 1698. On the invitation of William III, the Tsar visited Kensington Palace for tea and biscuits and after a convivial conversation, the King persuaded him to sit for the portrait.

Peter politely acquiesced and the renowned artist Sir Godfrey Kneller was ordered to drop everything and bring his brushes to the palace immediately. A contemporary newsletter erroneously reported the portrait was 'drawn to the life at full length in a Roman habit, a Marshall's staff in his hands and the Regalias lying by him and shipps storming a fort on the Sea Side' but in reality it depicted him in shining armour and cloak with his baton and regalia and a much less violent naval scene in the background. It was though a beautiful rendering of the Tsar, who looked every inch the cultured statesman.

Yet there is something of a discrepancy between the Peter in the painting and the young Russian ruler who caused something of a scandal during his little holiday on our shores.

The Tsar was a house guest of the famed English writer, gardener and diarist John Evelyn who happily handed over the keys to his pad in Deptford in south-east London, mumbled something about 'mi casa es tu casa' and headed off to find himself a hotel.

It proved to be a catastrophic mistake and after Peter had returned to Russia, Evelyn came home to find a scene of utter devastation. Almost every window of the building had been smashed, all the locks were broken, his paintings were riddled with bullet holes and his chairs and rather expensive staircase had been hacked to pieces for firewood. To rub salt into the wound, Evelyn's beloved holly bushes, the product of 20 years of loving cultivation, had been ruined after Peter and his drunken friends, who included the astronomer Sir Edmund Halley, decided it would be a jolly wheeze to push each other around in wheelbarrows and then dump the occupant into the prickly plants.

Such was the extent of the damage that Evelyn is said to have remarked it would be easier to dynamite the house than it would be to clean and repair it.

Peter apparently didn't even write to Evelyn to apologise for his antics, which is worth remembering if you happen to be in the Queen's Gallery at Kensington looking at the beguilingly regal image of the young, strikingly tall tsar.

THE PRICE OF MONEY
1699

The problem with a free market economy is the unpalatable fact there's always a recession or crash lurking just around the corner. The Wall Street Crash of 1929, Black Monday in 1987 and the recent banking crisis are all timely reminders that capitalism has its flaws and bankers are about as trustworthy as a cat in a dairy.

The 'South Sea Bubble' collapse in 1720 – a tawdry tale of British insider dealing and corruption – is generally acknowledged as the first modern financial crisis but a quarter of a century earlier the country found itself on the edge of a different economic precipice.

The problem was a flood of counterfeit coins. Public faith in the coinage was plummeting and the Government appeared powerless to solve the crisis.

'Great contentions do daily arise among the King's subjects in Fairs, Markets, Shops' wrote William Lowndes, the Secretary to the Treasury of Great Britain, in 1695. 'Persons before they conclude in any Bargains, are necessitated first to settle the Price of the Value of the very Money they are to Receive for their Goods, and if it be in Guineas at a High Rate or in Bad Moneys they set the Price of their Goods Accordingly.'

The man believed to be behind the bulk of this 'bad money' was one William Chaloner but despite their suspicions, the Treasury could not make anything stick. They needed their best man on the job and they found an unlikely champion in the shape of Sir Isaac Newton himself.

Yes, *that* Newton. The famed English physicist and mathematician may be better known as a leading light in the scientific revolution, author of the seminal *Philosophiæ Naturalis Principia Mathematica* and the man behind the reflecting telescope, but Sir Isaac also proved a rather adept at hunting down counterfeiters.

The intriguing game of cat and mouse between Newton and Chaloner began in 1695 when Sir Isaac was appointed Warden and Master of the Royal Mint. It was supposed to be an essentially ceremonial gig but when Chaloner published a pamphlet accusing Newton of incompetence and fraud in his new role, it was the straw that broke the camel's back and Sir Isaac retired to his offices at the Tower of London to plot his revenge. Quite why Chaloner decided to rattle Newton's cage is something of a mystery but if he hoped his public accusations would shine the spotlight away from his own criminal enterprise, he was sorely disappointed.

Newton quietly established a network of agents, spies and informers, despatching them across London to gather information about the epidemic of dodgy coins. Each time they identified a suspect, they were hauled back to the Tower for interrogation and slowly but surely, Sir Isaac built his case. It took him years but by 1699, he was ready to haul Chaloner before a court.

The previously untouchable crook knew the game was up. 'O dear Sir,' he desperately wrote to Newton after his arrest. 'Nobody can save me but you. O God, my God, I shall be murdered unless you save me.'

His pleas fell on deaf ears. He was convicted at his trial and on the morning of 22 March 1699, he was taken to the hanging tree at Tyburn and executed. Newton was not present for Chaloner's final moments, perhaps choosing to remain at the Mint inside the Tower and reflect on a job well done.

WHATEVER HAPPENED TO TIJOU?
1701

The interiors of Hampton Court are undeniably eye-catching but there is much to see outside the palace. Many visitors, of course, make a beeline for the world-famous maze but at the river end of the Privy Garden stands one of the palace's greatest treasures, the beautiful and ornate 'Tijou Screen'.

Commissioned by William III and installed in 1701, the stunning wrought-iron gates and railings were created by the French blacksmith and craftsman Jean Tijou and are testament to a rare talent indeed. Tijou's flamboyant style was the catalyst for a new movement in English metalwork and Hampton Court proved a picture-perfect setting for perhaps the greatest work of his career. Other examples of his metallic creations can be found in St Paul's Cathedral and Chatsworth House while he left his mark on the literary world in 1693 with the publication of *A New Booke Of Drawings, Invented and Designed by John Tijou*.

Tijou's personal life, however, was as complicated as his ironwork was elaborate and ground breaking and he remains one of the most enigmatic protagonists in the history of any of the five Royal Palaces. What little we do know about his story goes something like this:

Born in France, possibly in St Germain, he may or may not have trained in iron work at Versailles. He arrived in England after a spell working in the Netherlands but could equally have bypassed Holland altogether en route to Britain. He was married twice although it could have been three times. It really is impossible to be sure.

His marital background is particularly difficult to decipher. We don't even know the name of his first wife but the couple did have a daughter called Eleanor. His second wife, Anne, whom he married sometime after 1695, bore him three sons – Lewis, Thomas and Michael – before she died in 1708.

His third wife may not have been his wife at all. Her name was Elizabeth Winstanley and Jean met the new Madame Tijou when he was creating a weather vane for the lighthouse which her husband Henry was building on the Devon coast. Tragically, Henry, the weather vane and the lighthouse were all swept away by a freak storm and although no documents exist to prove it, it seems Jean and Elizabeth tied the knot after Henry's burial at sea.

Jeremy Kyle could have conjured up an hour-long special out of all that, no problem.

And yet the mysterious story of Jean Tigou does not end there. The last documentary evidence of him comes in 1711 in the records at St Pauls but after that he simply disappears from the face of the earth. There is a theory he returned to France but not once does he appear in any official register either side of the Channel and we have, in truth, absolutely no idea what happened to him.

We do know he was owed money for his work at Hampton Court. The death of his patron William II in 1702 probably threw the palace's whole invoice system into disarray but whether Tijou's disappearance was connected to the debt is a matter for debate.

SUBTERRANEAN REGICIDE
1702

As every gardener will testify, moles are the devil's spawn, ruining painstakingly coiffured lawns with their nocturnal excavations. The furry fiends are relentless diggers and are infuriatingly difficult to eradicate.

Annoying indeed but the miscreant mole that created an unsightly hole in the lawns at Hampton Court Palace in 1702 did much more than merely ruin the garden's aesthetic. The subterranean creature killed a king and changed the course of European history.

It was on 10 February that William III decided to take his favourite horse Sorrell for a canter around the grounds at Hampton. The jaunt, however, had tragic consequences when Sorrell inadvertently stepped into the aforementioned mole burrow and sent the King flying, breaking his collarbone as he unceremoniously hit the deck immediately after.

The royal doctors promptly set the bone but the 51-year-old King was neither a healthy nor robust man and in March he contracted pneumonia as a result of complications from his injury. William clung onto life for four days but on 8 March, the battle was over and he was dead.

His sister-in-law, Anne, assumed the throne while the Jacobites, the supporters of the rival royal dynasty of James II and his descendants, were over the moon and celebrated 'the little gentleman in the black velvet waistcoat' who had accidentally toppled the monarch.

The wider repercussions of the bizarre royal death were felt particularly keenly in the Netherlands. William had held sway over five of the Dutch Republics but when he joined the choir invisible, they were carved up by Prussia and France and the Dutch House of Orange of which he had been head was no more.

Modern visitors to St James' Square in London will notice the statute of William and Sorrell in the middle of the garden erected in 1808, a commemoration of the fateful moment the King's previously trusty stead placed his right rear hoof into the burrow and unseated the doomed monarch. There is no sign of our regicidal mole.

ORANGES ARE NOT
THE ONLY FRUIT
1704

The building industry is notorious for backhanders. You can't lay a single brick or pour a thimble of cement without someone 'getting a little drink' to set the wheels in motion and obtain the necessary permits and planning permission. Well, that's what some cynics say but that's probably because the roof on their loft conversion has started to leak.

Corruption in construction, however, does seem to have been somewhat rife in Queen Anne's brief reign in the early 18th century.

Despite Anne's 12-year stint in the hot seat, she never got round to any major works on any of the royal palaces but she was rather keen on building a new greenhouse and terrace at Kensington Palace where she could grow citrus trees and assorted exotic plants throughout the year and in 1704 plans were drawn up for her now famous 'Orangery'.

Responsibility for construction should have fallen to the Office of Works but an ambitious architect by the name of Sir John Vanburgh successfully muscled in on the action. Anne liked the cut of his architectural jib, approved his drawings and dropped the Treasury a polite note to say they'd be picking up the bill.

According to protocol, the master-mason Benjamin Jackson should have been in charge of the building work but he had something of a reputation for being 'creative' with his accounting. 'He is scandalous in every part of his character,' Vanburgh said. 'A very poor wretch and by many years regular course of morning drunkenness, has made himself a dos'd sott.'

Sir John turned to a mason by the name of Mr Hill to take charge but when he turned up on site with his hard hat and high vis jacket, he was shocked to find Mr Hill was conspicuous by his absence after a visit from some burly chaps and 'hints of what should befall him if he durst meddle with the master mason's business.'

Advantage Jackson. Another mason was employed but Vanburgh wasn't born yesterday and quickly realised the new fella was one of Jackson's men. After this, Sir John wearily decided to call it a day, accepting one of the immutable truths of life that you just can't get one over the union.

Anne's beautiful Orangery did get built but the bean counters at the Treasury nearly spoiled their spread sheets when the final bill for the work came in. Vanburgh had originally priced the job up at around £2,100 but Jackson submitted an invoice for £6,126, muttering vaguely about problems with the foundations, the price of materials and the cost of biscuits for the labourers.

Some things, it seems, never change.

THERAPY FOR THE MASSES
1714

Modern medicine is miraculous thing. Admittedly we may not have yet discovered a cure for the common cold but when you can buy tissues infused with Aloe Vera, what's the problem? We can, though, perform heart transplants, successfully reattach severed limbs and, most importantly, ensure ladies of a certain age can credibly celebrate their 43rd birthday well into their 50s.

Back in the 17th century there was more of a wing-and-a-prayer attitude to healthcare and this fingers-crossed approach was typified at the Banqueting House during James I's reign in the 'Touching for the King's Evil' ceremony.

Back then people really did put a lot of store in their monarchs. They were, after all, divinely chosen to be the boss and Mr and Mrs Joe Public trusted them to defend the country from filthy foreigners and ensure everything was tickety-boo. They also believed the king or queen could actually cure diseases.

The custom of 'Touching for the King's Evil' was the enactment of this erroneous belief, the practice of the people approaching the monarch to be touched and thus cured of their ailment. It had begun in England in the reign of Edward the Confessor and when the Banqueting House was completed in 1622, James moved the ceremony from the Chapel Royal at Hampton Court Palace to his new digs in town.

The medical problem James' subjects were afflicted by was the skin disease scrofula. Betrayed by a swelling of the lymph nodes in the neck caused by tuberculosis, scrofula these days can be effectively treated with drugs but back then it could be fatal and hundreds of desperate people would flock to the Banqueting House for a brief caress from the royal hand. In the reign of Charles II, the custom had become so popular that sufferers could only be brought before the King after they had applied for and been granted a special certificate.

During William III's stint (1689-1702) as top dog the practice was quietly shelved because Willy, a rather well known Protestant, believed it was nothing more than silly Papist superstition but when Anne was crowned Queen in 1702, the tradition was reinstated.

Anne died 12 years later and 'Touching for the King's Evil' once again fell out of favour. This time its decline was terminal and all subsequent monarchs were spared the ordeal of having to touch commoners. Figures for the clinical success rate of the bizarre custom are not available.

AN UNDIGNIFIED EXIT FOR ANNE
1714

Queen Anne may be synonymous with Kensington Palace but it's probably fair to say she wasn't particularly fond of the old Jacobean pile, scene as it was of so much heartache, misery and ultimately her own indecorous death.

During her lifetime, Anne had a staggering 17 pregnancies but most were miscarried or stillborn and only one child lived more than two years – Prince William, Duke of Gloucester, who died in 1700 aged 11 – and it was also where her beloved husband Prince George of Denmark breathed his last in 1708, succumbing to severe asthma and dropsy. 'The loss of such a husband,' she wrote, 'who loved me so dearly and so devotedly, is too crushing for me to be able to bear it as I ought.'

For 18 months, Anne stayed away from Kensington as she tried to come to terms with George's death but she was forced to return to the palace for her own last hours.

To describe Anne's demise as undignified would be an understatement. A gout sufferer, she had been unable to walk for much of the previous year and in July 1714, she suffered a stroke which robbed her of much of her speech and rendered her unable even to sign her own will. The end was nigh but there was unfortunately still time for the medical profession to heap more misery on the monarch as the doctors bled her, blistered her, shaved her head and covered her feet in garlic – all in full view of members of the royal court – in a misguided bid to save her life. They all failed and on 1 August, Anne died.

'I believe sleep was never more welcome to a weary traveller than death was to her,' wrote one of her doctors, John Arbuthnot, in a letter to Jonathan Swift.

Sadly we now know that garlic does nothing to block the inflammation caused by gout and Anne could have been spared at least one of the final indignities inflicted on her.

KENT'S KENSINGTON
CANVAS
1725

Everybody knows you have to get at least two quotes before getting any work done. Otherwise you're at the mercy of the Machiavellian machinations of unscrupulous traders and will only have yourself to blame if you end up paying hundreds for a new widget that cost £3.99 at B&Q.

A case in point is provided by the refurbishments of Kensington Palace undertaken by George I in the 1720s, proving that even Kings like to save a bit of money when the opportunity arises.

George took the throne in 1714 but when he took a look around Kensington for the first time, he found the Jacobean heart of the palace was in dire need of serious renovation. The noted Scottish architect Colen Campbell was given the job of redesigning the interior and Kensington was slowly transformed. There remained however the question of the decor. Campbell's new rooms needed decorating and thoughts turned to commissioning an artist to give the palace a suitably grandiose finish.

At the time Sir James Thornhill was the King's go-to painter. His work already adorned Blenheim Palace and St Paul's Cathedral and everyone assumed he would get the Kensington gig. Sir James duly submitted a quote for £800 for work required on the elegant Cupola Room at the palace and retired to wash his brushes, waiting for George to give him the green light.

He hadn't reckoned with Richard Boyle, the Earl of Burlington, who wasn't exactly a fan of Thornhill's work. Boyle got word to the King that an artist friend of his by the name of William Kent was looking for work and would he let him quote? George did and when the Yorkshireman, Kent, said he'd do the job for a mere £350 (cash in hand, no need to tell the VAT man or the missus), the King agreed.

According to contemporary reports, Sir James suffered a 'mighty mortification' when he heard the news that he'd been outmanoeuvred by the new kid on the block.

Kent re-created the coffered ceiling of the Pantheon in Rome in the Cupola Room. The work was finished in 1725 and, although it was suspiciously similar to what Thornhill had initially envisaged, intellectual property laws were hazy in those days and the plagiarism went unpunished.

George was so pleased with Kent's creation that he commissioned him to paint six more ceilings at Kensington over the next few years, as well as the palace's grand King's Stair. The Cupola Room though was the 'breakthrough' gig of his career and proof that money talks. Kent went on to be a garden designer. Remind you of anyone? (see The Artist Turned Agriculturist, page 59).

THE FERAL YOUTH
FROM HANOVER
1725

It is all too easy to dismiss the youth of today as essentially monosyllabic, surly and unkempt. They obviously don't help their cause with their insistence on wearing jeans that don't cover their backsides, their vacant expressions and impenetrable handshakes but they're not as bad as some of the more right wing press would have us believe. Probably.

They are certainly far more sophisticated than the young lad, christened Peter, who descended on Kensington Palace in 1725 on the instructions of George I and proceeded to make a complete mockery of the airs and graces of the Royal Court. Peter was literally a wild child.

The boy was discovered by villagers in woods near Hanover in 1724. Believed to be aged 11 or 12, he was living a feral existence, surviving on acorns, scampered around on all fours like an ape, was naked and was utterly without speech. They named him Peter The Wild Child and in an act of innate human kindness, promptly threw him into the local House Of Correction.

There he may have stayed but George happened to in Germany at the time, enjoying some R&R at his summer palace of Herrenhausen, and when the news reached him of the mute child who appeared and acted more like a beast than a person, he made Peter part of his household and brought him back to England and Kensington.

Peter was initially a sensation in England, albeit in the freak-show sense. His animalistic behaviour, his refusal to bow to the King and his apparent obsession of picking the pockets of guests in search of nuts, greatly amused polite society and everyone found the dubious spectacle a hoot.

But as with all oddities and curios, interest in Peter and his antics inevitably waned and it fell to the Princess of Wales, Caroline of Ansbach, to oversee his care. She instructed Dr John Arbuthnot (who had been physician to Queen Anne, see An Undignified Exit for Anne, page 83) to attempt to educate the youngster but his attempts to teach Peter to read or write or speak or even use a chamber pot or bed, essentially failed. He had 'a natural tendency to get away if not held by his coat' and it seemed the wild child could not be tamed.

The King died in the summer of 1727 and Peter's time at Kensington came to an end when he was subsequently sent to live with a farming family near Berkhamsted in Hertfordshire. The rural idyll clearly suited the boy from the forest and for the next 24 years he apparently contented himself with hunting for acorns.

In 1751 however he went missing. For three months there was no sign of him and it was not until a fire engulfed a jail near Norwich that he finally resurfaced as the prisoners were evacuated and Peter was identified as the famous erstwhile Kensington Palace lodger. No-one is sure how he got there but he was duly returned to Berkhamsted and, rather barbarically, fitted with a collar with his name and address burnt into the leather. Peter lived to a ripe old age, estimated to be 70, for which he probably had his natural foraging diet to thank.

It's a fascinating if sometimes disquieting tale but Peter's life story becomes more uncomfortable if we believe the modern theory that he suffered from the rare Pitt-Hopkins syndrome. It would certainly explain much of his behaviour and throws an unflattering light on the way he was treated by the Royal Court.

Visitors to the Palace today can still see Peter because he was immortalised by the artist William Kent (see Kent's Kensington Canvas, page 85) in his famous depiction of George's court which now hangs on the King's Stair. He is portrayed wearing a green coat and holding oak leaves and acorns in his right hand.

THE KENSINGTON
LOVE TRIANGLE
1727

It's safe to say the Georgians had a rather relaxed attitude to extramarital shenanigans back in the 18th century. It wasn't exactly the last days of Sodom and Gomorrah but there was definitely a sense of, shall we say, sexual licence that was perfectly acceptable in the Royal Court. Sometimes it was actively encouraged.

Which all led to a bizarre but intriguing love triangle that was enacted at Kensington Palace between George II, his wife Caroline and his mistress, Henrietta Howard. It's a story which a more puritanical audience might still struggle to comprehend.

Our central character is Henrietta. The daughter of a wealthy Norfolk landowner, the family fell abruptly on hard times when daddy foolishly decided to have a duel and got himself killed. Her mother passed away soon afterwards and it fell on Caroline to make a good marriage to provide for her siblings so she hastily tied the knot in 1706 with Charles Howard, the son of the Earl of Suffolk.

Sadly it was a bad choice as Charles proved to be a thoroughly bad egg, a 'drunken, extravagant, brutal' thug who terrorised his new wife and spent what little money they had gambling and in brothels. 'Thus they loved,' wrote one of Henrietta's friends, 'thus they married and thus they hated each other for the rest of their lives.'

The unhappy couple headed to Germany in 1713 to escape a series of bad debts and it was in Hanover that Henrietta met Caroline and was offered the job as her personal servant. Her job description however was quickly widened when George made no secret of his amorous attraction to Henrietta and she became his mistress with Caroline's blessing. According to Eleanor Herman in her book *Sex with Kings: 500 Years of Adultery, Power, Rivalry, and*

Revenge, George effectively bought hubby Charles off and the fumbling and cavorting could begin.

The 'threesome' arrived at Kensington Palace following George's Coronation at Westminster Abbey in October 1727 and the unusual arrangement continued despite Henrietta spending her evenings with the King and her days with Caroline in her role as servant of the Queen's bedchamber.

It was all frightfully civilised as Caroline calculated that Henrietta was a suitably discrete choice as royal mistress and that George could not be dissuaded from his out-of-hours pleasures anyway. There was also the problem of the King's notorious temper, which Henrietta rather than Caroline frequently bore the brunt of.

But affairs – like marriages – do not necessarily last forever and by the late 1730s it seemed that the cantankerous King was tiring of his bit on the side and the Royal Court suspected her position as his official mistress had become 'rather as a necessary appurtenance to his grandeur as a prince than an addition to his pleasures as a man.'

The clock was ticking for Henrietta but salvation came in the shape of the Grim Reaper in 1731 when her estranged husband's older brother left her money in his will. Two years later Charles himself went to an early grave and the time had come to forge a new future away from both George and Caroline at Kensington.

Henrietta remarried, built herself a house near The Thames in Twickenham and began her new life.

Henrietta and George were reportedly to meet one last time, many years later. 'In October 1760 a London traffic jam brought Henrietta's vehicle close to the coach of the king, 'whom she had not seen for so many years',' writes the historian Lucy Worsley. 'Henrietta recognised him immediately, but he looked back at her blankly. Although he had seen her every day for more than 20 years, George II had erased her from his memory.'

Whether Henrietta harboured any particularly fond memories herself of her relationship with the bad-tempered monarch is highly debatable.

A COMEDY OF BAD MANNERS
1730

Harold Pinter once flippantly remarked that his plays were about 'the weasel under the cocktail cabinet', a reference to the dark, unpalatable truths that invariably lie just beneath the veneer of polite society. He was talking about his own work but he could just have easily been discussing the opulent parties held at Kensington Palace during the Georgian era.

George II and Queen Caroline in particular were frequent hosts to famously grandiose social gatherings during the 1730s in the palace's Great Drawing Room. No expense was spared and their guests went to great lengths to ensure they looked their absolute best.

The 'uniform' for the ladies of the day was the 'mantua', an expansive coat-like dress with an enormous train. The dress was fanned out to seemingly impossible proportions by a whalebone hoop and while the women may have looked gorgeous, the mantua was far from the epitome of comfortable casual.

The real problem for these female party goers – Pinter's weasel, if you will – was, ahem, how to go to the toilet once they had got all trussed up. There were two accepted solutions but both came with embarrassing dangers.

The first was to use a small porcelain chamber pot called a 'bourdaloue' when the pressure on the bladder became too much. Think pretty china gravy boat and you're there. A lady in need of relief would simply place her bourdaloue between her legs and let nature take its course.

It was not even necessary to leave the room, although such behaviour could still repulse other revellers, as the wife of the French ambassador did at a series of shindigs at Kensington with the 'frequency and quantity of her pissing which she does not fail to do at least ten times a day amongst a cloud of witnesses.'

The other, seemingly more decorous avenue of relief for Georgian ladies was simply to retire to the little girl's room, although this was still a gamble if you happened to be in the presence of the Queen because you needed her permission to depart. If Caroline was not minded to grant you leave and you didn't have a bourdaloue handy, you simply had to cross your legs and hope and on at least one occasion at Kensington one of Caroline's ladies lost her battle with her bladder and involuntarily released a pool of urine which 'threatened the shoes of bystanders.'

Which probably put a bit of a dampener on the festivities.

GEORGE AND THE INDIAN CHIEF

1734

The Royal Palaces have opened their doors to a myriad of notable guests over the centuries from Continental kings and queens to courtiers, from archbishops to architects and from politicians to painters. Clapham Junction can't hold a candle to the palaces when it comes to footfall.

One of the most unusual visitors, however, has to be the Indian chief Tomochichi, who pitched up with a few of his scantily clad tribe at Kensington Palace in 1734 for a bit of a chinwag with George II. To be fair, he was invited.

The Chief was the grand fromage of the Creeks tribe from the south east of America and Tomochichi had recently proved rather useful in helping establish the British colony in Georgia. He had at the very least resisted the urge to scalp the soldiers at the garrison in the town of Savannah and as a token of George's appreciation, he was invited on-an-all-expenses paid jolly to Blighty.

Tomochichi and his entourage caused quite a stir at the palace when they pitched up in early August with their faces 'most hideously painted black and red' and a distinct lack of shirts, but an invite is an invite and George stuck to his promise.

The unprecedented meeting is described by George White in his book *Historical Collections of Georgia*, published in 1855. 'This day at one o'clock,' he wrote, 'Sir Clement Cotterell, attended by three of his Majesty's coaches, with six horses each, came to the Trustee's Office, for Georgia, in Old Palace Yard, and proceeded from thence with the Indian King, Queen, and Chiefs, and the interpreter, to Kensington Palace, where his Majesty received him seated on his throne in the Presence Chamber.'

It was the very definition of a culture clash but Tomochichi was undeniably a smooth operator and ingratiated himself with the King with a cracking speech which was music to George's ears.

'This day I see the majesty of your face, the greatness of your house and the number of your people,' he said. 'I am come for the good of the whole nation, called the Creeks, to renew the peace which long ago they had with the English. I am come over in my old days. Though I cannot see any advantage to myself, I am come for the good of the children of all the nations of the Upper and of the Lower Creeks, that they may be instructed in the knowledge of the English.'

Tomochichi sealed the deal by presenting the King with an eagle's feather – a Creek symbol of peace – and George duly remarked he would 'always be ready to cultivate a good correspondence between them and my own subjects.'

It had all gone jolly well but George's kind words must have rung rather hollow when the Creeks learned the British had ceded their tribal land to the newly independent United States in 1783 following defeat in the American War of Independence.

A RIGHT ROYAL ROW
1735

It's a fact of life that married couples argue. Domestic bliss is an impossible illusion to maintain forever and the more often a spouse insists on leaving the top off the toothpaste or throws his or her dirty washing on the bedroom floor, the more the martial tension inexorably rises.

Royal couples are not immune to such wedded woes and George II and Queen Caroline certainly had one hell of ding dong at Kensington Palace in 1735 that had probably been brewing for the 30 years since they'd tied the regal knot.

It all started when George sailed over to Germany for a spot of business. Caroline found herself at a bit of a loose end in his absence and decided to undertake a spot of reorganising in the King's Drawing Room. Specifically she decided she couldn't stand her husband's taste in art and removed his collection of Italian paintings including *Venus And Cupid*, a 16th century picture by the artist Giorgio Vasari which was based on an earlier work by Michelangelo.

The Queen ordered the Vice-Chamberlain, Lord Hervey, to adorn the newly bare walls with what she considered a fine collection of portraits of the Stuart royal family by the Flemish painter Sir Anthony van Dyck and the transformation was complete.

George hit the roof when he got home and demanded to know what the hell Caroline was playing at but it was her proxy, poor Hervey, who bore the full brunt of his displeasure as the King demanded his Italians painting were restored to their rightful place.

'Would his Majesty have the gigantic fat Venus restored too?' Hervey nervously enquired. 'Yes,' screamed George. 'I like my fat Venus better than anything that you have given me instead.'

The *Venus And Cupid* was quickly found and hung again, a rare example indeed of a husband actually winning an argument with his other half.

DOCTOR
ON FIRE
1737

Death is not a funny business. It's a time for sadness, solemn reflection and mourning but it doesn't mean you can't have a few laughs in the final hours before meeting your maker.

Queen Caroline evidently thought so in the days leading up to her frankly agonising death at Kensington Palace in 1737. Suffering from a complicated and extremely painful intestinal hernia, her final illness began with an attack of colic and violent vomiting and the doctors were summoned in a desperate bid to save her. Sir Walter Raleigh's famed 'cordial' was administered but proved ineffective and it was reluctantly decided that they would have to operate on Caroline to remove the blockage. There was, of course, no general anaesthetic in the 18th century and the Queen would be conscious during the procedure.

A doctor by the name of Randby was called to perform the ill-fated operation. Whether he was a prudent choice is debatable considering that the contemporary records reveal he was recently estranged from his wife 'after a quarrel' and may not have been in the right frame of mind for delicate surgery but Caroline certainly saw the funny side.

'Ranby [sic] the surgeon cut the Queen,' John Perceval, the Earl of Egmont, wrote in his diary. 'To show her contempt for the pain, she asked what he would give to be using his wife in the same manner.'

The deathbed comedy was still far from finished. 'At the same time old Bussiere,' continued Egmont's diary, 'who is near the age of ninety, and stood by Ranby to direct how to proceed in cutting her Majesty, happened, by the candle in his hand, to set fire to his wig, at which the Queen bid Ranby stop awhile for he must let her laugh.'

Without doubt, Caroline was a game old bird, but the end was nigh and she accepted her fate with typical stoicism. 'After fifty five,' she said after the unsuccessful surgery, 'a woman has no business to live.'

She urged her husband George II to remarry after she had gone and her final act was to return the ruby ring he had given her on her coronation day. 'This is the last thing I have to give you,' she said as she placed the ring on his finger. 'Naked I came to you, naked I go from you. I had everything I ever possessed from you, and to you, whatever I have I return.'

DAYLIGHT ROBBERY
1737

It was in the summer of 1982 that Michael Fagan broke into Buckingham Palace and got as far as the Queen's bedroom but his audacious act was not the first shocking breach of royal security in the history of the monarchy.

One of the most flagrant occurred in 1737 when George II was taking his customary stroll near the Round Pond in the gardens of Kensington Palace. Nothing seemed untoward until a man stepped out of the bushes, pointed a pistol at the King and told him to empty his pockets.

Somewhat apologetically, the robber explained he was a former soldier fallen on hard times and had only turned to a life of crime to support his family. He still wanted the swag but it was evidently important that George understood his motives.

The King handed over his rings, money, brooch and even the buckles from his boots. He then took out his watch and told his assailant he could have the timepiece and fob but the seal hanging from the chain, bearing his initials, had been a present from his late wife and he could not countenance handing it over.

Now don't forget our mystery man is still brandishing a loaded weapon. It's a delicate situation for both parties (potentially fatal for one) but the robber was nothing if not a pragmatist and told George that although he would still take the seal despite its sentimental value, he'd return to the same spot the following day and if the King came up with a hundred guineas in cash, he'd let him have it back. The one caveat was George didn't get the Old Bill involved.

The King wasn't really in a position to argue and returned to the scene of the crime the next day with the cash. He could, of course, ordered his royal guards to surround the spot and give the mugger a good going over before hauling him off to the Tower for some serious revenge, but he was a man of his word and he came alone.

So too did our former soldier. He brought the seal as promised, the deal was done and, according to the history books, the two men parted on good terms.

Bizarrely, this all-too-easy incursion into the palace grounds failed to see security significantly tightened and according to the diary of John Perceval, the first Earl of Egmont, two years later George was once again walking the gardens at Kensington when he was suddenly accosted by a man dressed in women's clothes. It was, it seems, something of a political protest as the cross dresser handed the King a letter full of anti-monarchy rhetoric and promptly disappeared.

After that, George decided it was safer to stay indoors.

A STICKY WICKET
1751

Cricket has always boasted a wealth of celebrity devotees and one of the earliest and most prominent of the sport's supporters was Frederick Louis, Prince of Wales, a man who simply adored the thwack of leather on willow.

Freddy moved to Britain from his native Hanover in 1727 when daddy became King George II. He quickly fell in love with the quintessentially English pastime and in September 1731 the records mention for the first time the 24-year-old Prince watching a match, a clash between Surrey and London on Kennington Common.

In August the following year the *Whitehall Evening Post* reported that Frederik attended a 'great cricket match' at Kew in July and in 1733 he was so enamoured with the game that he paid a guinea to each player at a meeting between Surrey and Middlesex which, in today's unfortunate climate of bribery and spot fixing, would certainly be frowned upon.

In the years that followed, there are numerous references to Freddy continuing both to watch and play cricket and the beautifully manicured gardens at Kew Palace frequently proved a convenient location for the Prince and his pals to hit a few sixes.

But his penchant for the game was perhaps to cost the Prince his life. The tragic event happened in 1751 when the Prince was enjoying a match at Kew only to be struck by the ball on the chest. At the time he thought little of it, nursing no more than a bruise, but the blow is believed to have led to an abscess on his lung. It subsequently burst and Frederik died in March at the age of 44 and was buried in Westminster Abbey.

In truth, no-one is absolutely sure what caused his death and we certainly cannot be 100 per cent confident that if it was a cricket ball that hastened his demise that it was struck at Kew. But it's a possibility and it also begs the question of whether any wag who attended his lavish state funeral was insensitive enough to remark that at least Freddy 'had a good innings.'

SWAN LAKE
1755

One of the enduring perks of being a member of the royal family is your birthday presents tend to eclipse the more mundane gifts the hoi polloi unwrap on their particular special day. When you're a royal weaned on the best of everything, an HMV voucher, novelty socks or even annual membership of the National Trust simply doesn't cut it.

Such was the dilemma in royal circles in the summer of 1755 as the Prince of Wales, the future King George III, neared his 17th birthday. Georgie's big day in early June obviously demanded a massive prezzie and his courtiers were certainly thinking big when they commissioned John Rich, the manager of Covent Garden, to design a boat in the shape of a giant swan that the Prince could enjoy on the lake in the gardens of Kew Palace.

'Wednesday 4 being the birth day of his Royal Highness the Prince of Wales a pleasure barge built by John Rich Esq was launched in the gardens at Kew and named the Augusta,' reported the June issue of the *Gentleman's Magazine*. 'It is formed in a taste entirely new and made to imitate a swan swimming. The imitation is so very natural as hardly to be distinguished from a real bird except by the size of it.

'The neck and head rise to the height of eighteen feet and the body forms a commodious cabin neatly decorated and large enough to accommodate ten persons and the feet so artfully contrived as to supply the place of oars which move it with any degree of velocity. The novelty of the design and the elegance of execution afforded particular pleasure to the Royal Family who were present.'

An engraving of the bizarre craft on the lake at Kew has survived and portrays a surreal scene of the enormous artificial swan on the water, towering over a number of presumably startled ladies on the bank.

THE SECRET
PORTRAIT PAINTER
1759

King George II would have absolutely hated Facebook and its users, incessant, obsessive need to upload pictures of themselves pulling silly faces, windsurfing or generally having the best time ever. George was not one of life's natural extroverts.

Luckily for him, Mark Zuckerberg was yet to revolutionise social media back in the 18th century and the King's privacy remained relatively intact. He was occasionally required to sit for obligatory state portraits, adorned head-to-toe in his royal bling, but he turned down countless requests from leading artists to sit for more informal pictures. He was the King and he could do as he bloody well pleased.

One painter by the name of Robert Edge Pine was determined to capture his monarch more *au naturel* and in 1759 hit on a cunning plan to get his man, hiding himself in a cupboard at the top of the grand staircase at Kensington Palace and waiting for the King to wander past, blissfully unaware he was to be an unwilling protagonist in a Georgian version of *Candid Camera*.

Quite what the palace security were playing at remains at a mystery but Pine's plan paid off when he spotted the King standing alone and deep in thought at the bottom of the stairs at the palace. Quick as a flash, Pine whipped out his pencil and paper and made a rapid sketch of the monarch which, in time, became a fully-fledged portrait – presumably after he'd extricated himself from his bizarre hiding place.

The painting's unconventional inception, however, is nothing in comparison to what happened next. Frederick Calvert, Lord Baltimore, the governor of the Maryland colony across the pond, decided he loved Pine's work and bought it.

Calvert intended to present the portrait as a gift to the Maryland settlers who were loyal to the Crown but he was ambushed by pirates in the Atlantic en route and after a hearty round of 'shiver me timbers' and 'avast me hearties', they half inched it.

The painting disappeared off the radar but a few years later a Royal Navy ship apprehended the very same pirates and recovered Pine's clandestine masterpiece. It was returned to England and in 1784 it was bought for 50 guineas by Sir John Griffin Griffin – so good they named him twice – and taken proudly back to his Audley End home in Essex.

Whether George was ever aware of Pine's subterfuge is not recorded but since he'd been dead for 24 years when Griffin made his purchase, he was probably past caring.

THE FINAL FLUSH
1760

Death, as the old saying goes, is the great leveller. The Grim Reaper is a staunch advocate of equal opportunities in the workplace and regardless of race, religion or views on either the JFK assassination or the Euro, we're all destined to cash in our chips sooner or later.

Even Kings eventually kick the bucket and so it came to pass in 1760 that George II's time was finally up after an eventful 33 years on the throne. Sadly for George, it was while perched on an altogether less stately throne that he eventually breathed his last. Yep, poor old George died on the toilet.

His sad and embarrassing exit came on the morning of 25 October at Kensington Palace. 'As there had been throughout so much of his life, an element of farce existed then,' wrote Clifford Brewer in *The Death of Kings: A Medical History of the Kings and Queens of England*. 'He rose at six in the morning, as he was accustomed, drank his chocolate and went to his close-stool. His valet de chambre heard 'a noise louder than the royal wind' accompanied by a groan and went into the chamber.'

He was not met by a pretty sight. George was slumped on the floor, having hit his head on the way down and although the alarm was rapidly raised, he was dead before his servants had managed to carry him to his adjoining bedroom. The post-mortem revealed the king had died from a rupture of the right ventricle to the heart.

At 76-years-old, George had certainly had a good innings and lived longer than any of his predecessors as monarch but his unceremonious end was surely not in the script.

A macabre footnote to the story comes a month later when the King was laid to rest with the pomp and ceremony befitting his illustrious station. The service was conducted at Westminster Abbey but old George had left instructions that his coffin should be buried close alongside his dearly departed wife Caroline and one side of each casket removed so the couple's remains could 'mingle' in the afterlife, inadvertently making a mockery of the 'til death us do part' line of their marriage vows.

KEW'S DISAPPEARING MOSQUE
1761

History isn't always an exact science. It's often based as much on interpretation and opinion as hard, indisputable facts and the claim to be Britain's first mosque is a perfect illustration of such diverse historical schools of thought.

For some religious scholars, the first mosque in Britain was established on Glyn Rhondda Street in Cardiff as far back as 1860 on what is now the site of the Al-Manar Islamic Centre. Others are adamant that first place of Islamic worship was founded in Liverpool in 1889 by the convert lawyer William Henry Quilliam while the Shah Jahan Mosque in Woking, built by Dr Gottleib Wilhelm Leitner, also claims to be the original.

The mosque once found in the gardens of Kew however predates them all by nearly a century and is a fascinating footnote in the palace's history.

The architectural development of the gardens was begun by Frederick, Prince of Wales, and after his untimely death in 1751 his widow Augusta continued the development, commissioning Sir William Chambers to build her a series of innovative buildings close to the palace.

Sir William knocked up a dazzling array of architectural curiosities including the Temple of Aeolus, The Pagoda and the Temple of Arethusa, which all still stand today. In 1761 he also designed and built the aforementioned mosque at the southern end of the grounds.

According to a 2003 UNESCO report on Kew, 'the mosque stood on a small mound near the Pagoda and consisted of one large central dome flanked by two smaller domes and minarets. The building was highly decorative and painted outside with Arabic text and inside with rococo style panels.'

There can be no doubt that Kew's mosque existed 99 years before Cardiff claims to have become a home to prayers. It's a moot point whether anyone ever actively worshipped inside Chamber's building and if it existed only in body rather than spirit.

The mosque is sadly not longer with us as Chambers didn't exactly have a long-term vision for his creation and used relatively cheap and flimsy materials. 'The whole was found to be so generally out of repair that it was thought proper to take it entirely down' reported *A Pocket Companion to the Royal Palaces of Windsor, Kensington, Kew and Hampton Court*.

The 18th century equivalent of the wrecking ball was swung in 1779 and Britain's 'first' mosque was no more.

LAURENS IN LONDON
1780

American tourists flock to London in their tens of thousands these days to sample the city's many famous attractions, descending on the Houses of Parliament and Buckingham Palace with a steely-eyed determination to savour the sense of history and empty the gift shops of beef eaters and double-decker buses.

In the late 18th century, however, the capital hosted an altogether more reluctant visitor from across the pond by the name of Henry Laurens, the first and still the only American to have been held prisoner in the Tower of London.

Laurens was a successful and hugely wealthy merchant, plantation owner and erstwhile slave trader who became a leading political figure in the American War of Independence. A fan of cricket, cream teas and queuing he was not.

In 1880 he was despatched to Holland on a hush-hush diplomatic mission but the Royal Navy ensured he never made it to the delights of Amsterdam, intercepting his ship off the coast of Newfoundland. Laurens was charged with treason and hauled off to the Tower.

Legend has it that the prisoner was brought in through the Tower Gate accompanied by a taunting chorus of 'Yankee Doddle Dandy' sung by the Warders but if Laurens feared he was in for an unpleasant stay in London, he was mistaken.

Money, of course, opens doors and while Laurens' vast fortune could not actually secure his release, it certainly ensured that a generous supply of champagne and fine wine flowed. America was winning the war and it was decided it would be unwise to make his porridge any harder than it needed to be.

He was also visited by a stream of merchants and businessmen desperate to make a new friend and trade with the soon-to-be-independent States and they invariably came bearing gifts – life, on the whole, at the Tower was surprisingly comfortable.

His incarceration eventually came to an end on New Year's Eve 1781 when he was released in as part of prisoner exchange deal that saw General Lord Cornwallis return to Blighty, while Laurens flagged down the next ship and completed his original journey to the Netherlands.

Two years later the Americans won the war and their independence when the Treaty of Paris was signed by all the protagonists. Laurens largely retired from political life after the hostilities but would tell all those who cared to listen that he knew of a very reasonable hotel in London should they ever visit England.

METHOD IN HIS MADNESS

1788

History has not been kind to George III. During his long reign, France were defeated in the Seven Years' War, he generously funded the Royal Academy of Arts and Napoleon was sent packing at Waterloo and yet the word that still springs to mind about the third Hanoverian king of Britain is 'madness'.

George wasn't mad though and it's now believed he was suffering from a metabolic disorder called porphyria, a nasty affliction with both physical and mental symptoms. Poor George suffered both.

The King succumbed to the first of his three severe bouts of illness in 1788 at the age of 50. The doctors described his affliction as 'an evil humour' but were at loss to explain his muscle weakness, abdominal pain, constipation, insomnia, agitation and violent outbursts. They prescribed leeching, a straight jacket (which George referred to as his 'hated waistcoat') and other ultimately ineffectual treatments but the King's 'madness' stubbornly persevered.

For the safety of his family, George was moved to the White House at Kew Palace but even during these dark days there were moments of endearing clarity from the monarch and one such example was unearthed when the kitchens at Kew, largely abandoned since the death of Queen Charlotte in 1818, underwent £1.7 million worth of renovations in 2007.

One of the treatments advised by the medical profession was regular hot baths to soothe the King's frayed nerves. There had long been stories that George would take these medicinal soaks in a tin bath in the kitchens of the White House amongst the hustle and bustle of the servants rather than in his grand state apartments, and, when the work began on restoring the kitchens to their former glories, the bath was discovered in a chimney opening.

The cynics might suggest a king bathing in the kitchens was merely proof positive of madness but in reality he chose the unusual location to spare the servants the arduous task of carrying countless buckets of hot water. George may have been suffering terrible bouts of mania but he still had the compassion to make life as easy as possible for the staff.

The King recovered from his first phase of porphyria in early 1789 and to mark his albeit temporary rehabilitation, he sat down for a meal of pigeon pie, veal, sweetbreads, pike, chicken, lamb, roast goose, pheasant and blancmange with his wife and children. Touchingly, George was presented with his knife and fork as he was no longer deemed a danger to himself or those around him.

Sadly his illness was to resurface twice more and he spent the rest of his life largely hidden from public view at Kew. A Regency was declared in 1811 and two years after the death of Charlotte, he passed away. His reputation as the mad monarch may persist but it's a reputation George scarcely deserves.

KANGAROOS AT KEW
1790

Over the years, the Tower of London has earned itself a reputation as the home to some of England's most exotic animal imports (see Beastly Fatality at the Tower, page 61) but in the late 18th century Kew Palace challenged its royal rival with a menagerie all of its own.

A paddock adjacent to Queen Charlotte's Cottage in the grounds of Kew was the scene of the makeshift zoo and although the resident black swans, oriental cattle or even buffaloes were hardly show stoppers, the arrival of the first kangaroos to reach our shores in 1790 certainly got tongues wagging.

The mob of kangaroos (which, fact fans, is the correct collective noun for a group of the Antipodean marsupials) was imported from Botany Bay in Australia, which had been 'discovered' by Captain Cook 20 years earlier. The local Aborigines quite reasonably pointed out the Bay had always been there but their protests sadly fell on deaf ears.

The new arrivals at Kew flourished despite the dramatic drop in temperature and by the early 19th century, the imported mob was 18 strong. They were joined in the Palace grounds by a beast called a quagga, a now-extinct relative of the zebra which George III had shipped over from South Africa.

The Kew Menagerie, however, was to prove a short-lived phenomenon and in 1806 Queen Charlotte ordered the royal gardener, Mr Aiton, to turn the paddock into a flower garden. The fate of the innocent kangaroos is unknown but there are records of a quagga in residence at London Zoo later in the century, so perhaps the unusual beast was reprieved.

THE TURNBULL TAKEAWAY

1798

Devotees of the *Mission Impossible* films will already be familiar with the accepted method of breaking into high-security facilities. Diminutive hero with dubious marital track record? Check. Improbable assortment of state-of-the-art ropes, pulleys and tools? Absolutely. Fleeting moment of tension when all appears lost but actually turns out peachy? You get the picture.

Those foolhardy enough to have attempted to get the better of security at the Tower Of London over the years, however, have employed distinctly more direct approaches.

Colonel Thomas Blood famously tried to half inch some of the Crown Jewels in 1671 by knocking out the Master of the Jewel House with a mallet but was apprehended before he even managed to get beyond the walls but a lesser-known story concerns one James Turnbull who decided to target the Royal Mint, housed at the Tower, in unashamedly agricultural style.

His two-dimensional 1798 heist went like this. Turnbull was a soldier deployed to guard the Mint but the Crown was obviously not paying him enough and he decided to top up his pension by helping himself to some of the guineas that were being cast. His approach was far from subtle.

'At nine o'clock he pretended to go with the other men to his breakfast but returned in a minute or two with a comrade named Dalton,' reads the report in the *Newgate Calendar*, a popular compendium of nefarious misdeeds and criminality.

'Turnbull went and clapped a pistol to the head of one Finch, an apprentice, who was left in care of the coining-room together with a Mr Chambers and demanded the key of the chest where the finished guineas were deposited. Mr

Chambers came up to interfere, when the prisoner levelled the pistol at his forehead, and pushed him into a passage leading to another room, in which he locked both him and Finch. He then opened the chest and took out four bags, containing two thousand, three hundred and eighty guineas, and escaped with them before an alarm could be made.'

To be fair, what Turnbull's plan lacked in sophistication and glamour, it made up for in terms of initial effectiveness and for a fortnight he eluded the Old Bill. A reward of one hundred pounds failed to unearth him and it was soon doubled in a desperate bid to locate the AWOL soldier.

The long arm of the law finally caught up with him on the south coast as he tried to charter a boat to France. By now, Turnbull was masquerading as a Mr Drake but the subterfuge failed to fool the authorities, probably due to his likeness to his 'wanted' poster.

'He wanted me to go to France, to Calais, Boulogne or Oftend,' said the boat owner, Mr Raine, at Turnbull's trial. 'But I would not go there for pleasure, unless he would go into Dover and get a pass to protect me and my people. Then I took him to Dover and we were three days and three nights before he was apprehended.'

The judge at the Old Bailey took a very dim view indeed of Turnbull's crime and he was sentenced to death. Three weeks later he was executed, a clear, if terminal, message to potential criminals that The Tower was absolutely off limits.

A GRIZZLY SIGHT
1811

If you've been paying proper attention you'll remember that the Tower of London became the unlikely home to a polar bear in the 13th century when the King of Norway gift wrapped – metaphorically rather than literally – the captive predator and shipped it off to the capital as a present for Henry III.

The big white fluffy fella, though, was not the last bear to turn up at the Tower and in 1811 King George III became the owner of a giant grizzly bear by the name of Old Martin, a gift from the Hudson Bay Company in Canada.

Privately the King complained he'd have preferred a new tie or a pair of socks but the bear had to be housed and another unusual member of the animal kingdom took up residence at The Tower.

The tale of Old Martin takes a fascinating turn five years later when a sentry on duty at The Tower was doing his rounds one night and was suddenly confronted by the ghostly apparition of a great bear coming at him with mischief in his eyes. According to the reports, the terrified guard lunged wildly at the spectral beast with his bayonet only for the blade to go straight through and lodge itself in a door frame. Legend has it the sentry died hours later, overcome by the sheer shock of the whole, ahem, grizzly business.

The ghost has never been seen since but many have drawn the obvious conclusion that the ghostly appearance was a manifestation of Old Martin from the afterlife, perhaps still struggling to come to terms with his abrupt relocation from the icy beauty of Canada to the urban charms of central London.

It's a captivating story but the problem is Old Martin wasn't actually dead when the guard met his untimely demise. The bear lived happily enough for 17 years at The Tower and when the Royal Menagerie was closed in 1835 and the animals transferred to

London Zoo, Martin packed his bags and headed off to Regents' Park, enjoying six more years of whatever captive Grizzly Bears enjoy doing before he finally went to visit the great salmon river in the sky.

So what did happen on that fatal night in 1816? Mulder and Scully used to tell us 'the truth is out there' but even they would struggle to solve this one.

MATERNITY MAYHEM
1819

When it comes to that magical, if painful, moment when a pregnant women is finally ready to give birth, the traditional advice from the medical establishment is to push. It's page one of the *Practical Guide To Midwifery* and even more important than the ubiquitous hot water and clean towels.

Back in 1819, however, as Princess Victoria of Saxe-Coburg-Saalfeld was poised to bring the future Queen Victoria into the world, the emphasis was very much not on pushing. The poor Princess was actively encouraged to hold on for as long as she possibly could.

The unusual prenatal situation arose as the reigning House of Hanover faced a succession crisis. George III was on the throne and although he had proven himself rather prolific in the bedroom, fathering 15 children, there were no legitimate grandchildren to continue the family line.

Step forward his fourth son, Prince Edward, Duke of Kent and Strathearn, who did the decent thing and married Princess Victoria in 1818. The newlyweds did their royal duty and quickly conceived and it seemed the House of Hanover was in rude health once again.

The problem was the couple were living in Germany and as Victoria neared the moment of truth, it was decided it would be prudent for her to give birth in England to legitimise the child's future claim to the throne.

The parents-to-be suddenly had to get a move on, speeding across Germany by carriage before boarding the fastest boat available to Blighty. They subsequently raced to London and Kensington Palace, arriving in the nick of time for the Princess to finally push and give birth to the future queen Victoria in the palace at 4.15 on the morning of 24 May 1819.

An interesting and unexplained footnote to the beginning of Victoria's long and intimate association with Kensington came a month later when she was christened.

The ceremony was conducted in the Cupola Room at the palace by the Archbishop of Canterbury. The usual dignitaries and courtiers were in attendance but rather than anoint the future Queen with water from a traditional font, a large gilded wine cooler was pressed into service as the Archbishop did the honours.

In later life Victoria was known to be fond of red wine mixed with scotch after a hard day's ruling, a throwback, perhaps, to her unusual baptismal vessel.

THE MOAT RAN DRY
1826

The eagle-eyed visitor to the modern Tower of London will notice the moat set in the outer wall of the Brass Mount in the north east corner isn't exactly overflowing with water. It is, in fact, bone dry and has been a H_2O free zone (apart, briefly, from the great Thames flood in 1928) for more than 150 years.

The moat was originally dug in the reign of Edward I in the late 13th century. It was made slightly redundant as a defensive feature during the Peasants' Revolt of 1381 (see Anarchy in the UK, page 18) when the guards left the Tower's front door wide open and for the next 400 years or so, the moat became little more than an expansive water feature due to the distinct lack of attacking armies, sieges and general fighting. By the 1830s however, the moat had become something of nuisance thanks to a fundamental design flaw.

The problem was the Tower's plumbing and the fact the latrines had been set up to empty directly into the moat. At high tide, the River Thames would inexorably wash the day's 'evacuations' back into the moat and the smell would engulf the poor residents of the castle. Something had to be done and it fell to Arthur Wellesley, aka the Duke of Wellington, to resolve the noxious dilemma.

The 'Iron Duke' had become the Constable of the Tower in 1826, some 11 years after famously giving Napoleon a bloody nose at Waterloo, and he was soon required to address the issue of the repugnant moat.

His first solution was to order the filthy silt to be skimmed off and taken away to Battersea as fertilizer for the local market gardens. It was certainly a green solution but ultimately ineffective and by 1841 the watery defence was so polluted that the Surgeon-Major was moved to describe how it was 'impregnated with putrid animal and excrementitious matter, emitting a most prejudicial smell.' Several of the Tower's soldiers subsequently died as a result of a cholera outbreak. A further 80 were hospitalised as the disease spread and Wellington resolved to find a permanent solution.

He decided that the moat had to be drained. The traditionalists bemoaned the fact that a moat without water would be missing the point but the Duke pressed on and by 1845 the work was finished and the old defence had been transformed into a fosse. The threat of another cholera epidemic was no more and the Tower's pungent reputation subsided.

DISH OF THE DAY
1827

Sexual tension can be a powerful thing and it certainly had a dramatic impact at Hampton Court in the early 19th century when a young solider by the name of Colonel Sir Horace Seymour came to visit and inadvertently left some of the female residents quite overcome with excitement.

Sir Horace arrived at Hampton in January 1827 and moved into an apartment in the southwest corner of the Base Court. By all accounts he was the very epitome of dashing and had been jolly brave at the Battle of Waterloo. He was also recently widowed and, by definition, back on the market.

The Colonel took to attending the Sunday service at the palace's Chapel Royal but on his first visit, he was alarmed when a young woman in a pew opposite suddenly fainted. Quick as a flash, Horace heroically jumped up, picked her up in his big, strong arms and carried her protectively back to his apartment until she was fully recovered.

Sorry, it all got a bit Barbara Cartland there, but the point is that Seymour was as gentle as he was gallant. You get the picture.

The following Sunday the same thing happened, although this time it was a different damsel in distress. On the third Sunday, there was another unexplained fainting fit.

By this stage Sir Horace's aunt, Lady Seymour, had had enough. She would not abide any more of this flagrant flirting with her little nephew and ordered a notice pinned to the door of the Chapel Royal.

'Whereas a tendency to faint is becoming a prevalent infirmity in young ladies frequenting this chapel,' it read, 'notice is hereby given that for the future ladies so affected will no longer be carried out by Sir Horace Seymour, but by Branscome the Dustman.'

We must assume that the aforementioned Branscome wasn't quite as dishy or dreamy as Sir Horace because the mysterious fainting stopped as abruptly as it had begun once Lady Seymour's edict was posted. Hampton Court's resident refuse collective operative was absolutely gutted.

THE GHOSTLY 'GREY LADY'
1829

With centuries of combined and frequently tragic history between them, it is little wonder the Royal Palaces have become a veritable hotbed of tales of ghostly sightings, spectral appearances and supernatural shenanigans. The stories of hauntings and things that go bump in the night are as numerous as the staff and visitors alike who have fled one of the historic buildings in various states of shock and terror.

We will explore some of the more modern supernatural sightings in later pages but if you were to play a ghostly version of Palace Top Trumps, the winning card would surely belong to Hampton Court and the chilling tale of Sybil Penn.

Penn was a member of Henry VIII's court in the 16th century. Her chief role at Hampton Court was childcare, looking after Henry's sickly son Edward after his birth in 1537 and although she outlived Edward, who died from what was believed to be a tumour at the age of 15, her days of service were not over and she went on to successfully nurse Henry's daughter, Elizabeth I, through a bout of small pox.

The Queen was so grateful to Penn for the devoted care of her younger brother that she was granted a pension and an apartment at Hampton Court and Sybil would spend her time sewing and spinning, skills for which she was renowned throughout the palace.

In 1562 Sybil herself succumbed to small pox and she was buried in the nearby Hampton Church. For more than 250 years that was the end of her story but in the 1820s the old church was demolished, Sybil's grave was relocated and a series of eerie and unexplained events began to unfold.

The first supernatural encounter happened in 1829 in the southwest wing of the palace. Various reports of the sound of a spinning wheel from behind a wall were received and when officials warily investigated further, an old, bricked-up chamber was discovered. An antique spinning wheel sat accusingly in the middle of the long-forgotten alcove.

Since then Sybil, christened the 'Grey Lady', has allegedly made regular appearances at Hampton Court, favouring the rooms she used to frequent and many who have spent the night at the palace have related how they awoke to been confronted with the spectral sight of a tall, elderly woman staring intently back at them.

As with any ghost story, whether you believe it or not is really down to your belief system. The cynics and scientists will readily debunk the idea of Sybil haunting Hampton as superstitious nonsense while others will find it very difficult to ignore the sheer weight of sightings. Real or not, however, Sybil is without doubt one of the Royal Palace's most frequently spotted ghosts.

THE ROMANTIC PARROT
1836

Dating was a very different game in the 19th century. Today it is all Match.com, Nandos and 'His and Hers' piercings but back in the days when Queen Victoria was a teenage princess, the whole business of finding a fella was an infinitely more rigid and at times bizarre experience.

Victoria was just 16 when her relatives deemed the time was right to begin the search for a suitable husband and as quickly as you could scream 'arranged marriage' her uncle, King Leopold of the Belgians, suggested his nephew Prince Albert was just the sort of chap they were looking for.

On 18 May 1836 Albert, his father Ernest, Duke of Saxe-Coburg and Gotha and his brother – who was confusingly also called Ernest – were invited to Kensington Palace to meet Victoria for the first time. For reasons known only to the Duke, he thought the gift of a tame parrot might foster a romantic ambience and for the duration of the meeting, Victoria and Albert attempted to flirt with each other over the bird's squawking.

The future queen, however, only had eyes for her Continental cousin. 'Albert, who is just as tall as Ernest but stouter, is extremely handsome,' she wrote in her diary. 'His hair is about the same as mine, his eyes large and blue and he has a beautiful nose and a very sweet mouth with fine teeth.'

Victoria's premature accession to the throne the following year (see Dressing-gown Diplomacy, page 129) and her subsequent marriage to Albert in 1840 is altogether another story but the parrot's part in the history of Kensington is far from over. Albert was Victoria's true love but she was rather fond of her exotic bird too, naming it Lory. 'It is so tame that it remains in your hand,' she wrote, 'and you may put your finger into its beak, or do anything with it, without it ever attempting to bite.'

So placid, in fact, was the bird that it happily sat for the artist Sir Edwin Landseer on more than one occasion at Kensington and his painting of the bird with three of the Queen's dogs, imaginatively entitled *Hector, Nero and Dash with the parrot, Lory*, is still part of the Royal Collection.

It may be an overstatement to suggest Lory paved the way for one of the Royal Family's most famous marriages but our feathered friend was certainly there to bear witness to the day Victoria and Albert first met.

DRESSING-GOWN DIPLOMACY
1837

We have already delved into the madcap birth of Queen Victoria at Kensington Palace in 1819 (see Maternity Mayhem, page 119) but her initial ascension to the throne some 18 years later was equally peculiar and certainly not the regal and stately occasion you might well have imagined.

The story begins in the early hours of 20 June, 1837, when William IV finally succumbed to a long-term illness at Windsor Castle and shuffled off this mortal coil. The king was dead and Victoria was the next cab off the rank.

The news of her uncle's demise had to be officially delivered to the new monarch and the Archbishop of Canterbury and the Lord Chamberlain, Lord Conyingham, were duly despatched to Kensington to tell the new Queen. They breathlessly arrived at the palace at four in the morning but Victoria's mother was not amused and stubbornly insisted her daughter should not be woken until at least six.

The clergyman and the Lord helped themselves to a much-needed coffee as they waited and at the allotted time, they trooped into Victoria's apartment at Kensington – now known as, you've guessed it, Queen Victoria's Bedroom – and imparted their portentous news. The future Queen, however, was not exactly dressed for the occasion.

'I went into my sitting room only in my dressing gown and saw them,' she later wrote in her diary, 'Lord Conyingham then acquainted me that my poor uncle, the King, was no more, and had expired at 12 minutes past two this morning and consequently that I was Queen.'

Her legendary, iconic 64-year reign had begun but Victoria's attendants were unsure how she would react to her sudden promotion and her governess, Louise Lehzen, was discreetly on hand with smelling salts but the Queen was made of sterner stuff and retained her composure.

Later that same day, Victoria met with her Privy Council at Kensington for the first time. It must have been a daunting rendezvous for the teenager and her nerves probably were not helped when her chair had to be raised up on a hastily assembled platform so her ministers could actually see her. Once again, though, she took it all in her stride, a measure of the self-control that would be a hallmark of her long and popular reign.

Becoming Queen did, however, come with perks and, after attending to pressing matters of state, Victoria quickly took advantage of her new status and ordered her mother's bed to be removed from her private chamber at Kensington. The poor girl had never slept alone and once mummy had been banished to an adjoining apartment, Victoria could finally enjoy whatever it is 18-year-olds get up to in their bedrooms.

HEROICS FROM THE MET
1841

The Tower of London, and the Jewel House in particular, have always prided themselves on being a tough nut to crack. When you house some of the world's most expensive and iconic bling, you've got to take precautions, and ever since the Crown Jewels were transferred to the Tower following their theft from Westminster Abbey in 1303, the royal collection has largely remained safely under lock and key.

There is, though, a fundamental flaw with such serious security. Namely, how the hell do you move the Crown Jewels in an emergency? Let's say, just hypothetically, if a ruddy great fire suddenly starts and threatens to engulf all that glorious gold, shimmering silver and assorted gemstones. The insurance company are never going to cover that lot, are they?

Such a potential disaster, of course, did rear its ugly head in 1841 when a stove flue overheated and the resulting flames licked their way to the Jewel House. It was certainly panic stations all round when Mr Pierse, a superintendent with the Metropolitan Police, arrived at the scene.

'It was deemed expedient to remove the Regalia and crown jewels to a safe place,' reported *Chambers Book Of Days*.

'Mr Pierse entered the building in question. To get hold the jewels was now the difficulty as these treasures were secured by a strong iron grating, the keys of which were in the possession of the lord chamberlain, or elsewhere deposited at a distance, and not a moment was to be lost.

'Crowbars were procured and a narrow aperture made in the grating so as barely to admit one person. Through this opening Mr Pierse contrived, with much difficulty, to thrust himself, and hand through from the inside the various articles of Regalia.

'Repeated cries were heard from outside, calling to the party within to leave as the fire was close upon them, Determined, however, to accomplish the behest which he had undertaken, Mr Pierse unflinchingly retained his post within the grating. The precious articles were all conveyed to the governor's house.'

A hero copper in anyone's book but according to Chambers, Pierse didn't exactly get the recognition his timely intervention probably deserved.

'Some public reward to Mr Pierse, who had thus gallantly imperilled himself to save the Regalia of the United Kingdom, would, we should imagine, have been a fitting tribute to his bravery. But no such recompense was ever bestowed.' He didn't even get his picture in the local paper.

A SURPRISINGLY POPULAR FUNERAL

1843

Royal funerals invariably spark a period of national mourning as the country comes together to mark the passing of a beloved member of the monarchy. The recent deaths of Princess Diana and the Queen Mother only served to underline the national impact of such sad events and the pomp and ceremony of the subsequent funerals are as magnificent as they are tearful.

The death of Prince Augustus Frederick, Duke of Sussex, at Kensington Palace in 1843 however, and the resulting public reaction, didn't quite follow the same template.

The sixth son of King George III, Augustus was not exactly a typical royal heir of the era. An asthma sufferer, he was the only one of George's boys who did not pursue a military career, he caused a scandal when he married for the first time in secret without seeking the King's permission and he dabbled with the idea of becoming a cleric in the Church of England. He spent the majority of his time in his apartments in Kensington, building up his library which would eventually fill 10 rooms and feature over 50,000 books.

Something of a wild card, then, but perhaps because of rather than despite of his idiosyncrasy, Augustus was hugely popular with the British public and when he passed away at Kensington at the ripe old age of 70, his death was greeted with widespread dismay and grief.

The people desperately wanted to pay their respects but Augustus had clearly stipulated in his will that he did not want a state funeral. Royal officials searched for a solution to keep everybody happy and they eventually decided to open up the Prince's apartments at Kensington, where had been laid out, to the public.

They simply could not have predicted the numbers who descended on the palace to say goodbye to Augustus. On one single day, a staggering 25,000 people turned up at Kensington to pay their respects and such was the throng that a temporary wooden staircase had to be hastily constructed leading from a second-floor window to ensure all the mourners were able to get in and out of the apartments safely.

Augustus' unusual 'exit' was not finished yet. The Prince had also decided he would not be buried in a royal cemetery and, according to his final wishes, he was laid to rest at the newly built Kensal Green Cemetery, an unconventional conclusion to what had certainly been an unconventional royal life.

MACABRE MEMORIES
OF NAPOLEON
1893

The Banqueting House may have begun its life in the early 17th century as a regal pleasure palace but nearly 300 years later the old pile was no longer a royal pad. Inigo Jones' grand design was unused and unloved and in 1893 Queen Victoria, disillusioned with paying the bills on a place she never visited, decided to wash her hands of Banqueting House.

She gave it to the Royal United Services Institute and after a bit of a kerfuffle over the initial plans to partition the building into offices, the Institute decided to establish a museum dedicated to military history and that kind of thing. Exhibits commemorating great British victories and campaigns were duly sourced and the museum opened to the public, an unashamed celebration of our national fighting prowess.

By far the strangest item on show, however, was not British at all but from the Continent. It was the almost-complete skeleton of Napoleon's famed horse, Marengo, and the story of how the Emperor's trusty steed found its way from the battlefields of Europe to central London goes something like this:

Marengo saw plenty of action during his life. The grey Arabian was imported to France from Egypt in 1799 as a six-year-old and although he was reportedly injured eight times in the line of duty, he safely carried Napoleon through the battles of Austerlitz, Jena-Auerstedt and Wagram.

His and the Emperor's luck famously ran out at the Battle of Waterloo in 1815 and Marengo was captured by Baron William Henry Francis Petre, who thankfully resisted the temptation to say 'for you horse, the war is over' before shipping his trophy back to Britain.

He was then sold to Lieutenant-Colonel Angerstein of the Grenadier Guards and put out to stud. Sadly Marengo apparently proved something of a flop with the ladies and at the age of 38, he joined the equine choir invisible. The Lieutenant-Colonel preserved the skeleton and donated it to Royal United Services Institute, who in turn placed old Marengo on display at the Banqueting House.

The more eagle-eyed reader will remember the gift was an 'almost' complete skeleton. For reasons known only to himself, Angerstein decided to remove one of the hoofs and turn it into a rather grizzly snuff box for the Brigade of Guards, but other than that, Marengo was the whole package.

The Institute's museum at Banqueting House was closed in 1962 but you can still see Marengo in all his skeletal, albeit three-hoofed glory at the National Army Museum in London.

GIRL POWER AT THE PALACE
1898

Hampton Court has welcomed many diverse, interesting house guests over the centuries. Most have been genteel, thoroughly well-behaved and, perhaps, a little dull but all that changed at the end of the 19th century with the arrival of Princess Sophia Alexandra Duleep Singh.

The daughter of Maharaja Duleep Singh and Bamba Muller, Sophia also happened to boast Queen Victoria as her godmother and in 1898 the Princess was granted a grace-and-favour apartment in Faraday House at Hampton Court. If the other minor female royal residents thought they were about to welcome another recruit to the bridge club or crochet circle, they were to be sorely disappointed because Sophia was an ardent suffragette and she caused quite a stir at the palace.

She began by handing out leaflets furthering women's issues outside Hampton Court but as a leading light in the Women's Tax Resistance League and the Women's Social and Political Union, Sophia was also prepared to get her hands dirty and was to the fore alongside Emily Pankhurst on 'Black Friday' in November 1910 when 300 marched on Parliament in protest at the MPs' reluctance to pass the legislation required to extend the right to vote to some women. The protest turned ugly and many of the women were roughed up by the thoroughly ungallant policemen on duty.

It was, though, her stance against the inequalities of the tax system that really thrust Sophia into the public spotlight and in 1913 she was hauled in front of a judge (not for the first time) to explain why she wasn't sending her cheques to HMRC. The bailiffs had already turned up and confiscated a pearl necklace comprising 131 pearls and a gold bangle studded with pearls and diamonds in lieu of payment but Sophia was unrepentant.

'When the women of England are enfranchised I shall pay my taxes willingly,' she defiantly announced. 'If I am not a person for the purposes of representation, why should I be a fit person for taxation? Taxation without representation is a tyranny. I am unable to pay money to the state as I am not allowed to exercise any control over its expenditure.'

By now the suffragette movement was gaining real momentum and there was even talk of an attack on Hampton Court to make a bold statement of intent. It never materialised but the rumours did put Sophia in an awkward position, as *The Evening Standard* gleefully pointed out in June 1914.

'Do Princess Sophia Duleep Singh and [her sister] Princess Catherine Duleep Singh, and Lady Wolsey, all of whom have enjoyed the hospitality of the King at Hampton Court Palace, approve of the burning of that historic residence, which has been marked for destruction for some time? Princess Sophia Duleep Singh and Princess Catherine Duleep Singh are housed as the King's guests at Hampton Court Palace, yet the Princess has given £51 and collected £6.7s in the last year to aid a union many members of which intend to burn Hampton Court Palace at the first opportunity.'

Quite what the other residents of made of all this is a matter of conjecture but her commitment to the cause never waned and when, in 1928, Pankhurst died, it was Sophia who was elected as her successor as president of the Suffragette Fellowship. Sophia herself passed away in August 1948 but it was not before she had helped make a lasting impression on the political landscape of the country.

A CASUALTY OF WAR
1915

War has an uncanny knack of breeding fear and suspicion. The famous Second World War maxim 'Careless Talk Costs Lives' is legendary and the pervasive sense of misgiving and distrust was just as endemic when Britain crossed swords – and artillery and tanks – with Kaiser Wilhelm II in the Great War.

The public were urged to keep their eyes peeled for German spies and when someone pointed the finger at a businessman by the name of Franz Buschmann, the authorities were convinced they'd uncovered a clandestine minion of the German empire at work.

He was quickly arrested, put on trial, convicted and packed off to the Tower of London to await execution.

The problem with the story is the evidence against Buschmann couldn't even be described as thin. In fact, it was so flimsy it wouldn't have looked out of place in Beyonce's wardrobe and beyond his suspiciously Teutonic name, there appears to have been no other crime to answer. What we do know is Buschmann was born in Paris, his father was a naturalised Brazilian and his mother was Danish.

His pleas of innocence however fell on stubbornly deaf ears and he became the latest in a long line of prisoners to spend their final, dark days within the stone walls of the Tower. 'Is it really true he will never come back to me?' wrote his distraught wife. It was.

He spent his last night alive playing his violin into the small hours and when a guard arrived in the morning to escort him to face his fate, Buschmann kissed the instrument. 'Goodbye,' he said. 'I shall not want you any more.' He was executed at the East Casemates Rifle Range inside the Tower by firing squad.

PHILLIP'S MUSICAL MAYHEM

1930s

Edward VIII once described Kensington Palace as an 'aunt heap' due to the number of minor female royals who had taken up residence in the former home of William and Mary. It was perhaps a slightly unkind depiction of the palace but it is true that Kensington was brimming with titled ladies in the 1930s.

One of the distinguished residents at the time was the Dowager Duchess of Milford Haven, a granddaughter of Queen Victoria, and one of her regular visitors to the palace during the school holidays was her young grandson, Phillip. For those of you not intimately acquainted with royal genealogy, that's the same Phillip who made an honest woman of Princess Elizabeth before she became queen, then embarked on a part-time and not wholly successful career in the diplomatic corps.

By all accounts, the young Phil was a boisterous chap and the serene peace of Kensington would often be disturbed by his penchant for playing his trumpet at full volume. The Dowager was not impressed and Phillip had to be frequently admonished for upsetting his elderly aunts in the neighbouring apartments with his noisy recitals.

The Prince was to become synonymous with Buckingham rather than Kensington Palace in later life but he did return to the scene of his childhood trumpeting on 19 November 1947, spending the night with his grandmother before leaving the following morning for his marriage to Princess Elizabeth, his second cousin once removed.

Before his very public nuptials in Westminster Abbey, Phillip is said to have fortified himself with a quick gin and tonic at

Kensington with his best man, the Marquis of Milford Haven, before heading off to face his fate.

A black-and-white picture of the Prince in his full ceremonial military dress leaving the palace still exists. Adhering to royal protocol, he left his G&T indoors.

DEFYING THE LUFTWAFFE
1940

By anyone's standards, Hampton Court Palace is a piece of prime real estate. Picturesquely nestled on the banks of the Thames and blessed with extensive and beautifully manicured gardens, it's far enough away from the chaos of central London and yet close enough to town to commute. Estate agents would commit bloody murder to get the listing.

It has, of course, never been on the market but, according to legend, one Adolf Hitler was an eager, prospective resident of Hampton Court during the Second World War, planning to make the palace his new British HQ had his planned invasion of Blighty been successful. There's actually no hard evidence to prove that the Fuhrer did have designs on Hampton, but, if the story was true, one or two errant Luftwaffe pilots would surely have been facing a firing squad.

It was in September 1940 that the Luftwaffe mounted one of their nightly raids on London. In sharp contrast to modern laser guided missiles, bombing was far from an exact science in those days and whether intentionally or in error, the German bombers dropped some of their deadly cargo on Hampton Court.

The building was showered with incendiary devices and as soon as the alarm was raised, the palace's resident firefighters were mobilised to fight the flames. The problem was some of the bombs had landed on the roof while the firemen were firmly on terra firma.

Mercifully there was a contingent of wardens stationed on the roof and quick as a flash, they kicked the incendiary devices onto the ground where they could be dealt with. There was some minor fire damage to a number of the grace-and-favour apartments on the East Front of the palace but, in essence, Hampton Court had escaped unscathed.

Whether Hitler ever learned of the near miss or whether he would have lost any sleep had the building been razed to the ground is a moot point but it's certainly true that thanks to the footballing prowess of palace staff, Hampton Court's long history was preserved.

Sadly Kensington Palace was not quite as lucky as its royal cousin during the Blitz, suffering major damage to the Queen's apartments in October 1940 after another Luftwaffe raid.

Once again, however, it could have been much, much worse had it not been for the courage and alacrity of the palace caretaker, the only person in the building at the time, who heroically removed a number of unexploded bombs before they had time to wreak their intended havoc.

THE NAZI AND THE SLEEPING PILLS

1941

The Tower of London has been no stranger to celebrity inmates over the centuries but one of the highest profile and ultimately most mysterious 'guests' has to be Rudolf Hess, the deputy Fuhrer of Nazi Germany and erstwhile right-hand man of Adolf Hitler.

His journey from the Fatherland to a cell at the Tower in 1941 was as circuitous as it was bizarre and one of the strangest episodes of the Second World War.

Hess flew incognito from Germany and parachuted into Scotland after his Messerschmitt crashed, landing in a field 30 minutes from Glasgow and breaking an ankle in the process. He was arrested by a local ploughman by the name of David McLean, who politely informed the German he'd do him a serious mischief with his pitchfork if he didn't do exactly as he was told, and Hess was duly carted off to the nearby Marryhill Barracks.

In May 1941 he was transferred to London and the Tower where he became something of a celebrity, signing autographs for the warders. One of his signatures still hangs in the warders' bar today.

Hess spent three nights in the Tower but his historic surroundings were apparently not to his liking and he needed sedatives to get to sleep. Local pharmacist H A Rowe was called and he prescribed a mixture of potassium bromide and choral hydrate 'with flavouring' to help the nervous Nazi get his 40 winks.

The original prescription was put up for auction in 2009 and fittingly it was The Royal Armouries which made the winning bid for its museum housed in the White Tower.

During his brief sojourn at the Tower, Hess was publicly disowned by Hitler who apparently knew nothing of his little trip.

Adolf claimed his former best mate was mentally unstable, stripped him of all his titles and rank and Hess was later tried for war crimes at Nuremberg and imprisoned in Spandau jail in Berlin until his death by suicide in 1987.

The mystery of Hess' flit remains however. Most assume he had embarked on an impromptu peace mission behind Hitler's back but since all government records of the bizarre incident are subject to the Official Secrets Act until 2017, we cannot yet be certain.

KRAYS INCARCERATED
AT THE TOWER
1952

They loved their mum, did Ronnie and Reggie Kray. They certainly weren't quite so fond of George Cornell and Jack 'The Hat' McVitie, but when it came to maternal devotion, the notorious East End gangsters were undisputed mummy's boys.

Mrs Kray had the dubious distinction of bringing Ronnie and Reggie into the world in 1933, presumably blissfully unaware of the violent havoc they would subsequently wreak, but 19 years later the twins would pay for their unhealthy obsession with Violet with a spell 'inside' at the Tower of London at Her Majesty's pleasure.

The 1950s was a decade in which National Service was still in operation and in February 1952 the Kray boys got their papers to join the Royal Fusiliers. The following month the twins reported for duty to the Yeoman Warder at the Tower and the trouble really started.

A staff sergeant showed the boys around their new dormitory but they were not impressed. 'We don't like it here,' they announced. 'We're off home for some tea with our mum.' The sergeant politely informed them that it didn't work like that, was punched in the face for his trouble and Ronnie and Reggie headed back home to Vallance Road in Bethnal Green for a spot of Earl Grey and petit fours with mummy.

The British Army, however, is nothing if not persistent and promptly sent the Old Bill round to frogmarch the boys, who'd spent the night staring menacingly at revellers in a dancehall in Tottenham, back to the Tower.

A court-martial ensued. The twins employed a cunning defence, arguing that it was impossible for the hapless sergeant to prove which one of them had actually struck him, but the court called their blatant bluff and sentenced each of them to seven days in the Guard House.

Ronnie and Reggie were among the last miscreants ever to do porridge at the Tower but sadly their first taste of prison didn't exactly curb their criminal tendencies. They went AWOL from the Fusiliers for a second time after their initial punishment but it was back on Civvy Street that the twins really made their mark. Unfortunately, it was invariably on the face of anyone who got in their way.

THE FAIRER SEX
2007

The issue of women in the workplace has been a thorny one ever since the fairer sex began vocally questioning their second-class employment status. The 20th century saw women score a number of notable victories in the battle for equality at work with the passing of The Sex Disqualification (Removal) Act in 1919 and the Equal Pay Act 50 years later but the fight goes on and institutionalised chauvinism has not been defeated yet.

One of the more recent victories for working women came in 2007 when Moira Cameron was unveiled as the Tower of London's first ever female Beefeater, a mere 522 years after Henry VII first founded the army unit as his personal bodyguard and protectors of the Crown Jewels. Those dreaming of female emancipation at the famous old Tower had had to be extremely patient.

Officially known as the Yeomen Warders of Her Majesty's Royal Palace and Fortress, the Tower of London and Members of the Sovereign's Body Guard of the Yeoman Guard Extraordinary (which really is an awful mouthful), the Beefeaters had provided more than five centuries of testosterone-dominated royal service before Moira's arrival and her appointment after 22 years in the Forces with the Women's Royal Army Corps and the Royal Corps of Signals was headline news.

'Working here at the Tower of London is absolutely amazing,' she said after her first week in the new job. 'I feel so privileged to be here and it's great to be in the uniform at last. I'm still getting used to wearing it but it certainly makes you stand very straight.'

Moira beat off competition from five male candidates to get the coveted £20,000-a-year post, which comes with accommodation at the Tower, and joined 35 other resident Beefeaters for the ceremonial role. At the time of going to press, she was still regaling visitors with tales of the Tower's many myths, legends and key events on the hour-long tours that prove so popular with tourists but it would be a lie to say her historic arrival didn't ruffle one or two feathers with some of her more 'old-fashioned' colleagues.

Sadly, the unfortunate business concluded with an unseemly disciplinary procedure, an employment tribunal and some rather poor publicity but you can't make an omelette without breaking a few eggs. It would be churlish to point the finger of blame but let's just say some people don't like change.

THE NEARLY NUDIST GARDEN
2011

It was in 1990 that Hampton Court first staged it's now world-famous Flower Show. The old royal palace welcomed the hordes of professional and amateur horticulturists alike with open arms and the annual celebration of flora and fauna began.

And all was well until 2011 when there was a blatant breach of protocol. It was quite a risqué break with tradition to be perfectly honest and somewhat undermined the show's reputation as a bastion of good, clean family fun.

The offending exhibition was called 'The Naked Garden' and was the brainchild of television landscape designer David Domoney. The idea was to display the exposed beauty of plants and their all-important roots, growing them in see-through Perspex pots without soil.

'The garden showcases some of the world's most striking plants in a completely different light and we're delighted to be recognised for creating something the garden world loves,' said Domoney after his garden was awarded a silver medal. 'Using clever glass technology, which allows the plants to grow soil-free in glass containers, garden lovers are able to discover a whole new side to the world of plants.'

All perfectly decent and proper you may cry but the Flower Show is still showbiz and it was decided the Naked Garden needed a schtick and after a three-second brain storm, it was agreed to draft in a male and female model in their birthday suits to generate a bit of welcome publicity.

To be fair, they weren't quite naked, as the eye-candy figures were both bedecked with strategically placed bouquets of flowers to preserve their modesty, but by Hampton Court's modest standards, it still a represented a rather racy stunt.

The Duchess of Cornwall was one of the higher profile visitors to the Flower Show in 2011 but declined to comment about the cheeky blurring of the lines between naturalism and naturism.

THE TOWER'S BADGES
OF HONOUR
2012

Security for the 2012 Olympics in London was tighter than a miser's grip on his wallet. Thousands of police and military personnel were mobilised to keep the Games safe and the feverish celebrations that greeted the success of Mo Farah and Jessica Ennis aside, the Olympics mercifully passed off calmly and without major incident.

One of the less publicised aspects of the security operation at the Games, however, was the safe storage of the 4,700 gold, silver and bronze medals destined to hang around the necks of the winning athletes. It was, of course, absolutely imperative that nobody meddled with the medals.

Step forward the impregnable vaults at the Tower of London, home to the Crown Jewels and arguably the safest place in the country to deposit such a precious delivery.

Designed by British artist David Watkins and fashioned from more than eight tonnes of gold, silver and copper at the Royal Mint in South Wales, the haul of medals was dropped off at the Tower in July, three-and-a-half weeks before the start of the London Games, with strict instructions that they should not be disturbed under any circumstances.

'For an athlete, winning an Olympic or Paralympic medal represents the conclusion of thousands of hours of training and reaching the highest level in sport,' said London 2012 chairman Lord Coe after dropping off the medals. 'The victory ceremonies then provide the moment they can truly celebrate their success. It's great that the medals will be kept safe and secure at the Tower of London until then.'

The redoubtable old Tower did its job and the medals were finally unlocked when China's Yi Siling clinched the first gold medal of the Games when she was victorious in the women's 10m air-rifle event.

Ironically, the Tower's temporary treasure was nowhere near as valuable as you might think despite the high security. The 302 gold medals on offer contained just 1.34 per cent actual gold (the rest was 92.5 per cent silver and 6.16 per cent copper) while the bronze medals contained no bronze whatsoever.

BONFIRE BURGLARY
2012

The World's Dumbest Criminals is a compelling Darwinian televisual study of greed and incompetence overcoming intelligence and common sense. It's also hilarious when the idiotic thieves panic, trip over their shoelaces and headbutt the cashier's security screen.

You would have thought it would take a particularly stupid criminal to attempt to rob the Tower of London in the modern era. It wasn't unheard of back in the day (see The Turnbull Takeaway, page 115) but in a contemporary world of motion sensors, alarms and infrared cameras, it would surely require the most audacious of burglars to try to break and enter at one of the most tightly guarded locations in the country.

These obstacles, however, did not perturb one particular felon on Bonfire Night in 2012 when he successfully scaled two of the Tower's external gates and ransacked a box containing keys to the drawbridges, conference rooms and restaurant.

'Security was a total shambles,' a source breathlessly told *The Telegraph*. 'The burglar climbed over the Front Gate then got over another gate and found a metal box with the keys inside. The box is supposed to be kept locked at all times but it was open. It went from bad to worse. Guards saw him but could not leave their positions to chase him. They tried to radio a night watchman but got no response.'

Mercifully the crook did not manage to get his hands on the Crown Jewels or anything else of value but there was still a financial cost as embarrassed Tower officials were forced to change the compromised locks at a cost of thousands of pounds.

The Metropolitan Police dutifully launched a massive manhunt for the burglar but the story took another twist when it emerged that the intruder had actually been spotted by the security control centre and the night guard was dispatched to apprehend him. He got there within three minutes of the incursion but instead of slapping on the cuffs, the guard inexplicably escorted him to the front door and let him go.

'A staff disciplinary procedure is underway to address this issue,' confirmed a sheepish spokesman for Historic Royal Palaces in the wake of the incident, but the daring crook was never caught. 'We have carried out an internal investigation and have concluded that our well-established security systems and procedures are robust,' the spokesman continued. Robust, in this context, meaning as leaky as a sieve.

DON'T WAKE THE BABY!
2013

The birth of a new baby into any family is a joyous, emotional event but the arrival of a new royal *bambino* invariably sparks national celebration as Brits abandon their traditional sense of decorum to welcome the latest prince or princess into the world. Many excitable well wishers are even drawn to camp outside the hospital, patriotically descending on the scene of the delivery armed with deckchairs and thermoses, manically waving teddy bears for the benefit of the hordes of TV cameras that have also set up shop outside the maternity ward.

The arrival of Prince George of Cambridge in July 2013 was no different. Thousands of royalists and media alike besieged St Mary's Hospital in Paddington for news of William and Kate's first baby and when the birth of the third in line to the throne was confirmed, there was much rejoicing as well as fevered news reporting.

The happy occasion, of course, demanded a more formal commemoration and following protocol, the next day there was the traditional Royal Salute across the capital to greet little George. London duly reverberated to the sound of thunderous guns, which did at least temporarily drown out the sound of the shrill shrieking still to be heard from the die-hard royalists at the hospital. Whether the noise also woke the new prince is unknown.

The simultaneous shots were fired by the King's Troop Royal Horse Artillery when they unleashed a 41-gun salvo in Green Park at two o'clock. At the same time, the Honourable Artillery Company (HAC), the City of London's army reserve regiment, supplied their own 62-shot salute from the Gun Wharf at the Tower of London with three 105mm light guns, two of which saw action during the Falklands war.

One of the smallest divisions of the Army, the HAC is responsible for all royal salutes fired from the Tower and, although it is a territorial rather than full-time unit, it does boast an interesting and unique claim to fame among the Armed Forces. The HAC is in fact the oldest-surviving regiment in the British Army.

Although it can trace its history as far back at 1087, it was officially born in 1537 when the regiment received a Royal Charter from King Henry VIII. Then known as the 'Fraternity or Guild of Artillery of Longbows, Crossbows and Handgonnes', the HAC has since actively served in both World Wars and was part of the NATO forces in Bosnia during the 1990s. It also holds the odd distinction of having fought for both the Parliamentarians *and* Royalists during the English Civil War.

The Tower's sharp shooters, however, miss out on the honour of being the world's oldest army unit by just 31 years, that distinction going to the Pontifical Swiss Guard in the Vatican who have been guarding Popes, with varying degrees of success, since 1506.

Members of the HAC who are to be assigned royal-salute duties undergo extensive training before they are let loose on the big guns although day one does tend to focus on the importance of loading blanks rather than live shells.

BIBLIOGRAPHY

BOOKS

Experience the Tower of London, Brett Dolman, Susan Holmes, Edward Impey & Jane Spooner, Historic Royal Palaces, 2010

Discover Kew Palace, Sebastian Edwards, Historic Royal Palaces, 2006

Discover the Banqueting House, Susanne Groom, David Souden, Jane Spooner & Sally Dixon-Smith, Historic Royal Palaces, 2011

The Banqueting House, Simon Thurley, Susanne Groom & Susan Jenkins, Historic Royal Palaces, 1997

Kensington Palace Essential Tales, Margaret Dorman, Rhiannon Goddard, Alexandra Kim, Joanna Marschner, Deirdre Murphy, Lee Prosser & Lucy Worsley, Historic Royal Palaces, 2011

Discover Kensington Palace, Margaret Dorman, Sebastian Edwards, Alexandra Kim, Joanna Marschner, Deirdre Murphy, Lee Prosser, David Souden & Lucy Worsley, Historic Royal Palaces, 2012

Hampton Court Palace: The Official Illustrated History, Lucy Worsley & David Souden, Merrell Publishers Limited, 2005

Kew Palace: The Official Illustrated History, Susanne Groom & Lee Prosser, Merrell Publishers Limited, 2006

Tales From The Tower, Fiona Jerome, Think Publishing, 2006

Architecture of England, Scotland and Wales, Nigel Jones, Greenwood Press, 2005

WEBSITES

www.ancientfortresses.org

www.archaeology.co.uk

www.archive.org

www.biographybase.com

www.british-history.ac.uk

www.castlewales.com

www.englishhistory.net

www.historysheroes.e2bn.org

www.hrp.org.uk

www.infobritain.co.uk

www.kew.org

www.londonist.com

www.paranormal-encounters.com

www.pbs.org

www.publicbookshelf.com

www.royal.gov.uk

www.royalarmouries.org

www.royalmint.com

www.royalmintmuseum.org.uk

www.royalcollection.org.uk

www.secret-london.co.uk

www.shahjahanmosque.org.uk

www.shakespearesengland.co.uk

www.shakespeare-online.com

www.theanneboleynfiles.com

www.thetudortattler.com

www.web.archive.org

www.yourlocalguardian.co.uk

AND NOW FOR SOMETHING EVEN STRANGER!

9781906032760   9781906032913   9781907554476

The Strangest Series has now introduced even stranger delights for its readers. With *The Ashes' Strangest*, *World Cup's Strangest* and *Olympics' Strangest*, fans of this unique and extraordinary series can delve even deeper into the world of the bizarre and utterly ridiculous with these special sport-related *Strangests*. A great read no matter where you are, these fascinating books highlight the bizarre, weird and downright bonkers events, characters and locations of each particular sport.

Just don't read them all at once though – you might start acting all peculiar! You have been warned.